Creating Fire & Brilliance in Fabric, Ste

GEMSTONE QUILTS

MJ Kinman

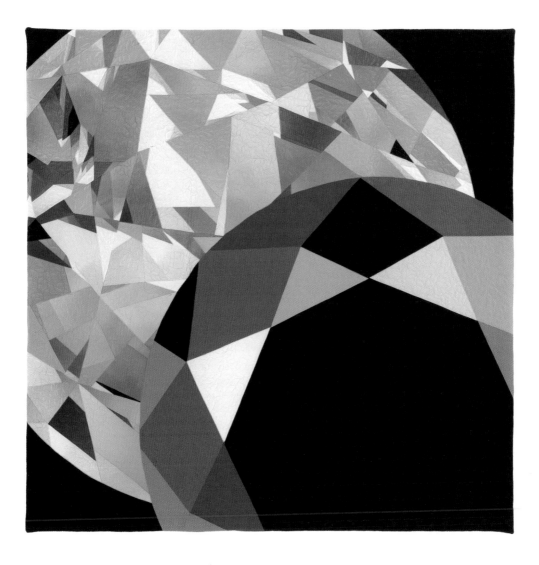

Text copyright © 2020 by MJ Kinman

Photography and artwork copyright © 2020 by C&T Publishing, Inc.

Publisher: Amy Barrett-Daffin

Creative Director: Gailen Runge

Acquisitions Editor: Roxane Cerda

Managing Editor: Liz Aneloski

Editor: Kathryn Patterson

Technical Editor: Debbie Rodgers

Cover/Book Designer: April Mostek

Production Coordinator: Tim Manibusan

Production Editor: Jennifer Warren

Illustrator: Kirstie L. Pettersen

Photo Assistant: Gregory Ligman

Photography by Estefany Gonzalez of C&T Publishing, Inc., unless otherwise noted

Published by C&T Publishing, Inc., P.O. Box 1456, Lafayette, CA 94549

Library of Congress Cataloging-in-Publication Data

Names: Kinman, M. J., 1962- author.

Title: Gemstone quilts : creating fire & brilliance in fabric, step by step / MJ Kinman.

Description: Lafayette, CA : C&T Publishing, [2020]

Identifiers: LCCN 2020013020 | ISBN 9781617459450 (trade paperback) |
ISBN 9781617459467 (ebook)

Subjects: LCSH: Quilts--Design. | Quilting--Patterns. | Gems.

Classification: LCC TT835 .K5236 2020 | DDC 746.46/041--dc23

LC record available at https://lccn.loc.gov/2020013020

Printed in the USA

10 9 8 7 6 5 4 3 2 1

Dedication

For my beautiful mother, Bess

Acknowledgments

Thanks to the C&T Publishing team who made this book a dream come true for me. From the time I picked up my first C&T quilt book 30 years ago, I knew I wanted to be part of your family.

I am grateful to all the Gem Affiliates who are teaching gem patterns and to the students who have taken my classes. You have taught me so much and have made me a better teacher, pattern designer, and quiltmaker.

Thanks to the artists who have allowed me to include their work in my book: Karen M. Bailey, Linda Fisher, Annette Fry, Julia Graves, and Jimeen A. Thurston. Your creativity and skills are amazing!

Thanks to Laurie and Simon Watt (Mayer & Watt) for allowing me to find inspiration in their gorgeous collection of colored gemstones, and to Geoffrey Watt

Unheated seafoam sapphire
Photo by Geoffrey Watt (Mayer & Watt)

for his spectacular gem photos. Thanks also to Douglas Mays of Wild & Petsch, the Smithsonian Institution's Mineral Sciences Department, and the Gemological Institute of America (GIA) for allowing me to use images of their stunning gems.

Special thanks to Tony Bennett (Tony Bennett Photography), Cindy and Bill Brundage, Nikki Caruso, Jeanne Delpit and BERNINA of America, Deborah Edwards and the Northcott team, Cynthia England, Kerin Ferrin, Jeannde Ford, Marissa Ghavami and Healing TREE (Trauma Resources, Education & Empowerment), Lindsey Grand and The Warm Company team, Desiree Habicht, the Hastings College Jackson Dinsdale Art Center (JDAC), Mary-Jeanine (MJ) Ibarguen, the International Quilt Museum (University of Nebraska-Lincoln), Victoria Johnson, Asher Katz and the Jacquard Products team, Annie Koenig, Judee Konen, Kelly Nagle, Gay Nordvik, the Paintbrush Studio Fabrics team, Cliff Patrie, Rhonda Pierce and the SCHMETZ Needles team, Jason Prather and the Sulky of America team, Lyvonn Reese of Threads Retreats, Luana Rubin and the eQuilter.com team, Rob Samuels (Chief Operating Officer of Maker's Mark Distillery), Sandee and Lynn Schulwolf, CJ Sturtevant, Shelley and Bernie Tobisch and the Acorn Precision Piecing Products team, Deena White, and Kelly Zuber.

This book is dedicated to Bess Liversidge, my beautiful mother, best friend, and favorite quiltmaker. Thank you for your love then, now, and forever.

Thanks and much love to my sisters Elizabeth, Mary, and Brenda. I adore your strength, humor, and loving kindness.

I could not have started—let alone finished—this book without the love and support of my husband, Joe Kinman. Thank you, my love, for your patience, kindness, faith, guidance, encouragement, and steadfastness.

Contents

My Story

The French director Jean-Luc Godard once said, "A story should have a beginning, a middle, and an end … but not necessarily in that order." The challenge of telling our own story is that beginnings, middles, and endings are happening all at once. And often the relationships between events aren't clear. My story is no different. I'm still on the journey, but perhaps I can provide a little perspective on the adventure so far.

Fancy zoisite
Photo by Geoffrey Watt (Mayer & Watt)

Communion, 55˝ × 77˝, 2013,
from the Angle of Repose series

The Beginning of the End

My desk phone, which had been ringing all morning, started ringing again. This time I didn't pick up. I'd had enough.

Sitting in my cubicle on the eighth floor of a corporate office tower in Louisville, I finally decided to pay attention to the message my head and heart had been sending me for months: *Get out and get out **now***. The thoughts made no logical sense, because I was where I thought I'd always wanted to be. I was working as a project manager for a Fortune 100 company, engaged in challenging work, and making more money than I ever thought possible.

So why was I so profoundly miserable?

Joy and Fear

This book is the result of choosing joy. I don't claim to know much about joy, but I know quite a bit about living with its opposite—fear.

There truly are only two states: fear and joy. Fear encompasses all things that have to do with anxiety—anger, hate, greed, bullying, worry, and sadness. Fear is instinctual. It's triggered in our amygdala, the reptilian brain that resides at the base of our skull, by stimuli that frighten us.

Joy, on the other hand, encompasses a world of love, kindness, mercy, grace, compassion, contentment, certainty, and gratitude. Joy is a choice. It is the willingness to act on the realization that we are divine and whole, regardless of where we are or what's happening in our life.

If you envision these two emotional states as a physical stance, joy is open. The posture is receptive, engaged, poised for the dance. The posture of fear is a defensive posture—closed, defending against danger. You cannot be in these two states at the same time. You must choose one or the other.

And, as I learned sitting in my corporate cubicle, if you remain in the defensive posture of fear for too long, your joy-starved soul just might rebel.

Yellow-green sunstone
Photo by Geoffrey Watt (Mayer & Watt)

Walking Away from Fear

Tajiki spinel
Photo by Geoffrey Watt (Mayer & Watt)

My career ambitions were sparked early, driven by my family's painful disintegration after my father's business failed. As a 12-year-old, I watched my family crumble. From that experience I learned that if you become unemployed, horrible things happen—bankruptcy, foreclosure, addiction, constant fighting, divorce. I know now that a host of other factors contributed to the chaos, but back then the equation seemed clear: Lose a job; disaster happens. That fear propelled me to start working at 13 and drove me for the next 40 years.

The fear of failure also created in me a fixation on perfection. I wanted things in my life and work to be perfect, even in my quilting. To use a quilting analogy, all the points in my life had to match *perfectly*. Talk about pressure! The pursuit of perfection leaves little room for joy. And the cruel thing about striving for perfection is that it's an illusion. It simply doesn't exist. Perfection is an unworthy goal, precisely because it is unattainable.

You can imagine then how unreal it was when I decided to quit my corporate gig. I realized that I had become a "project monster," not a project manager. Fear, anxiety, and frustration met me every day I walked into the office. It felt awful. I began to wonder what would happen if I cast all that aside and chose joy instead. What was the worst thing that could happen if I quit my job and focused on the thing that brought me the most joy—my quilting?

Once that idea wormed its way into my brain, I couldn't let it go. I was disengaging more and more every day at work until I just didn't care anymore. I knew my soul had left the building and I needed to do the same.

Leaving my job was the scariest, but truest, decision I've ever made. The day after I quit, joy returned to my life. I had no idea what the next steps would be, but I chose to trust that the universe would show me. I am so grateful that I have a marvelous husband who supported my decision and agreed to carry the load as I waited for my future to unfold.

Finding Joy

I learned how to quilt with my beautiful mother, Bess. She and I loved quilts and joked that quilting was in our cultural DNA. Mom was raised in the Mennonite faith, and her great-great-grandparents were Amish from the Wayne and Holmes County area in Ohio.

When Mom told me about a friend of hers named Gay who made gorgeous quilts and was willing to teach us the basics, I jumped at the chance. Each Wednesday for a few months, Mom and I showed up at Gay's house and learned to make templates, mark fabric, use a rotary cutter, match points, and piece curves. I quickly finished a little five-block wallhanging, hung it on a wall in my apartment, and immediately bought more fabric. I was hooked. I had discovered my joy!

A few years later, a flier for a performance at the Kentucky Center for the Arts arrived in my mailbox. I was struck by the image on the cover—a sparkling gemstone illuminated by a shaft of light. As I stared at the image, I wondered if I could transform it into a quilt design. After all, the shards of light and color bouncing through the gem were just straight lines.

As I studied the gemstone, the faceting pattern began to emerge, and I realized there was definitely a struc-ture to the chaos of color. The next step was figuring out how to make a pattern in which all of the pieces would be different shapes. What material would I use for templates? How would I know which color to use for each tiny piece? And once cut apart, how would I piece them back together in perfect order?

Over the next few years, I took classes and read everything I could about piecing techniques. Jane Hall, Dixie Haywood, Ruth B. McDowell, and Paula Nadelstern were some of my favorite teachers. It all came together, though, when I saw a picture of Cynthia England's spectacular award-winning quilt, *Piece and Quiet.*

MJ's first quilt, a five-block sampler, 1987

Columbia Artists presents

ACADEMY OF ST. MARTIN IN THE FIELDS

Inspiration for MJ's first gem quilt, 1991
Photo by Tony Bennett Photography

MJ's first gem quilt, *Solitaire*, 1997

Rubellites
Photo by Geoffrey Watt (Mayer & Watt)

Cynthia's description of freezer-paper piecing answered all my questions. I could draw my pattern on the smooth side of the paper, assign each piece a unique identifier code and color code, cut it up, and iron it to the right side of fabric. The waxlike substance on the reverse side would adhere to the fabric but easily release without leaving a residue. Seven years after receiving that image of a gemstone, I completed my first gem quilt.

Over the next twenty years, I continued to make gem quilts while working in the nonprofit world and subsequently, in the corporate world. I was focused on climbing the career ladder, doing what I thought I was supposed to do, never dreaming that quiltmaking might one day be a full-time endeavor. That is, until the day I gave my notice and jumped off the career ladder.

For the first year or so, I was adrift. Not sure how to make my dream a reality, I dove into everyone else's dream. Through one of those projects, I met Desiree, a woman who had created a successful career out of her love of quilting. When she agreed to coach me, we worked together to shape my vague dreams into reality.

Choosing Joy

It's a daily exercise to choose joy. With each new project I've launched, my old friend Fear invariably appears and tries to cozy up to me. I have to constantly confront her and command her to leave.

It's not easy. Fear is a hard habit to break. A good analogy to dealing with fear is like yoga practice. Some days you nail the poses and other days you can't find the balance to save your life. The important thing is to keep at it. Keep choosing joy.

Let me share an example of how easy it is for me—for all of us—to choose fear instead of joy. On August 21, 2018, a day arrived that should have been one of the most joyful of my career. But instead of choosing joy, I caved to fear. Rob Samuels, Chief Operating Officer and the third generation of Samuels family leadership, had commissioned a "bourbon diamond" quilt for their on-site restaurant, Star Hill

Provisions. They had provided the dimensions for the space it was to occupy, even going so far as to provide an architectural elevation.

I worked on *Maker's Flame* for several months, and on the day it was to be installed, my husband and I drove down to present the finished work. However, on the way to the distillery, my old friend Fear appeared and started badgering me. "It's too big. It's not big enough. They'll want their money back. You've spent the money!" Joe tried to calm me down, but Fear wasn't buying it, and sadly, I was listening to her instead of him.

When we arrived at the distillery, I unwrapped the nine-foot quilt and laid it on a table. The staff who were supervising the installation looked at the quilt, then at each other, and then at me. "We thought it would be bigger," they said.

I thought I was going to be sick.

Instead I asked them, "So tell me more about what you're thinking?"

Maker's Mark Distillery installation, *Maker's Flame* (Loretto, Kentucky)
Photo by MJ Kinman

"Rob said it would be bigger. In fact, he said it would fill the entire sixteen-foot wall space. We were worried how we were going to hang such a huge quilt. So … we're actually *happy* that it's not as big as he said it would be."

They liked it! I thought I was going to faint. (Clearly, I hadn't yet developed the stomach for commission work.) Following the installation, I learned that Rob loved the piece.

See what I did there? I robbed myself of joy. Instead of relishing every moment of presenting and overseeing the installation of my first big corporate commission, I stole the joy from the day all because I imagined the worst.

Here's another situation in which the worst thing *did* happen, but I made a conscious decision to choose joy anyway. A few months after the Maker's Mark lesson, I was in Alberta, Canada, presenting a couple of trunk shows and classes. Not having shipped quilts across the US/Canada border before, I didn't get them out early enough. Even before I arrived in Edmonton, my wonderful host for the first trunk show called me with the bad news: "The quilts aren't going to make it in time."

I panicked, wept, and called my coach for advice. The show must go on! I decided that, even though I was angry at myself for making such a bone-headed mistake and heartsick for the 100 people who were planning to attend my presentation, I was going to *choose joy instead.* My reasoning: If I was a hot mess before and during the presentation, not only would I rob myself of the joy of being with all those wonderful people, I would rob them, too. And that would be pure larceny.

The day of the trunk show came, and I explained the situation to the audience. A giant groan of disappointment hit me like a wave. I said, "I know. Me, too. Here's what I want to do for you …" And I told them about choosing joy.

I dove into my presentation and gave them everything I had for 90 minutes. I had juiced up my original presentation the night before with more pictures of my quilts, more stories, and lots of information about making bourbon. At the end of my talk, I remember that a few people (maybe most of them?) gave me a standing ovation. By consciously choosing joy, I had helped to spread it to others. See how that works?

La Brezza, The Good Fairy, a reproduction of the original 1950s work by Oscar Mattison in Cave Hill Cemetery (Louisville, Kentucky)
Photo by Tony Bennett Photography

Joy and Quilting

I have decided to let go of fear in my quilting practice, too. It's so easy to get hung up on perfect points, perfect color choices, or whether people will appreciate your work. That's why I decided to create quilt patterns where precision isn't a priority. I want my patterns to bring joy, not fear.

What I love about my diamond designs is that there are no points to match and no "right" color choices. *Light doesn't follow quilters' rules.* The important thing about gems is that they can sparkle and glow in a million different ways. You can do whatever you want with your gem, because it's *yours.*

Perfection is not a priority with the techniques that I'm going to share with you in this book. And once you let go of perfection, it's much easier to invite joy back into your quilt studio.

Thank you for your interest in and enthusiasm for the gems. I wish you peace and joy. Shine on!

—*MJ*

How to Use This Book

Let me state clearly and emphatically right up front: I am a *lousy* sewist. Seriously. By the time I sit down at my sewing machine, I've probably broken a dozen or more cardinal sewing rules even before I flip the power switch. If you're searching for tips on how to be an expert sewist, please return this book. However, if you want to learn how to transform your inspiration into a gorgeous quilt, read on.

My goal for this book is to introduce you to a powerful technique that you can put in your quilting toolbox—freezer-paper piecing techniques. I use these techniques to create quilts inspired by gemstones. Your inspiration may be different—landscapes, flowers, animals, portraits, or abstract art. Regardless, the flexibility of freezer paper can help you transform nearly any idea into a dazzling quilt.

Part I focuses on the lessons I've learned about design during the past twenty years creating my gem quilts. I'll talk about how the concepts of "cut, color, and clarity" guide my design decisions. I'll also share what I've learned about online applications and tools that will help you create compositions that delight.

Part II is devoted to technique. You'll learn how to create your freezer-paper template, including all the visual clues that you'll need to piece your design. As I describe the techniques, you'll have a chance to practice them by working on a sample project I've designed especially for this book. The gem that inspired the project is from the collection of Laurie and Simon Watt, my friends and international gem dealers. It is a gorgeous Mozambique purple garnet. I've named the project *Lovely Laurie* in honor of my friend. Finally, I'll wrap up the section with a discussion about quilting and finishing your gorgeous creation.

In Part III you'll find a gallery of my work and work created by students who have successfully used freezer-paper piecing techniques to create beautiful quilts.

Enjoy!

Teal sapphire
Photo by Geoffrey Watt (Mayer & Watt)

MJ in studio
Photo by Tony Bennett Photography

PART I

GEMS AS DESIGN INSPIRATION

*Photo by
MJ Kinman*

CHAPTER 1

The Casting Call: Discovering the Personality of Gems

Bicolored tourmaline
Photo by Geoffrey Watt (Mayer & Watt)

Blue-green tourmaline
Photo by Geoffrey Watt (Mayer & Watt)

We all know the type. Gorgeous, glamorous, glorious. They light up a room and sparkle in the spotlight. They love the red carpet and snag all the awards.

You might think I'm talking about last year's Academy Awards winners, but I'm not. I'm talking about the quilts that give you whiplash when you spot them in your peripheral vision, the quilts that demand your attention from across the room. I'm talking about the quilts you dream of making!

While your inspiration may be landscapes, portraits, still life, or abstract images, my inspiration for the past twenty years has been gemstones. I've spent hours looking for images of dazzling stones to use in my work.

Whether they're making a statement with a bold splash of color, flirting with a flash of brilliant light, or sporting an amazing cut, these lovely gems have taught me much about creating work that delights. My hope is to inspire you to look at your subject matter in new ways and, using freezer-paper piecing techniques, bring out the bling in your own compositions.

Bicolored watermelon tourmaline
Photo by Geoffrey Watt (Mayer & Watt)

Aquamarines
Photo by Geoffrey Watt (Mayer & Watt)

Three of the Four C's: Cut, Color, and Clarity

Experts in the gem industry commonly describe a gemstone using the *Four C's*: cut, color, clarity, and carat. Understanding the first three—cut, color, and clarity—is key to creating a quilt that sparkles like the gem that inspired it.

Lavender zoisite
Photo by Geoffrey Watt (Mayer & Watt)

Organized Chaos: The Cut of a Gem

When people first see my gem quilts, they typically ask one of two questions: "How long did it take you to make this quilt?" or "How in the world do you piece these things?" The second is a much easier question to answer.

My gem quilts are built block by block. In that regard, they have a lot in common with traditional quilts. The only difference between my quilts and a typical traditional quilt is that my blocks are wonky shapes. It's all based on the gem's cut, its faceting pattern. Once you spot the underlying structure of a gem, you can piece it using freezer paper.

Facets: Windows into the Heart of a Gem

Facets are the flat, polished surfaces of a gem. Gem cutters are the magicians who meticulously slice off portions of a gemstone to unlock its brilliance, color, and luster. More than any other factor, the precise positioning of these facets determines the beauty of the stone.

Think of facets as windows and mirrors. The facets on top of a gem function as windows, welcoming light into the heart of the gem. The facets on the bottom function as mirrors, bouncing light around the interior of the gem until it bursts back out through the top in a blaze of light.

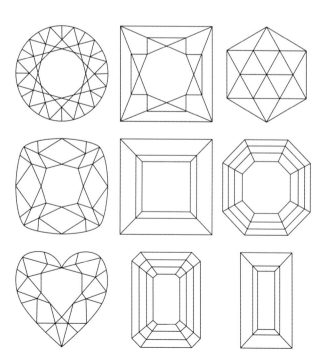

Samples of faceting patterns used today
Illustrations based on images by Gemological Institute of America (GIA)

Round brilliant-cut diamond
Photo by Gemological Institute of America (GIA)

There are literally thousands of faceting patterns in use today. Some are highly branded, while others remain unnamed. In order to introduce you to the basic anatomy of a faceted gem, however, I'd like to introduce you to the most common and probably the most beloved faceting pattern in the gem world: the round brilliant cut.

Crown   The crown is the up-facing portion of the gemstone. It consists of the table facet, the kite (or bezel) facets, star facets, and upper girdle facets. These are the windows into the heart of the gem.

Girdle   The girdle is the thin band that separates the upper (crown) facets and the lower (pavilion) facets.

Pavilion   The pavilion is the lower portion of the gemstone. It consists of the lower girdle facets, the main pavilion facets, and a culet (the tip of the stone). The pavilion acts like a hall of mirrors, scattering light around the interior until it angles back up through the crown to dazzle your eye.

Diagram of round brilliant-cut facets
Illustrations based on images by Gemological Institute of America (GIA)

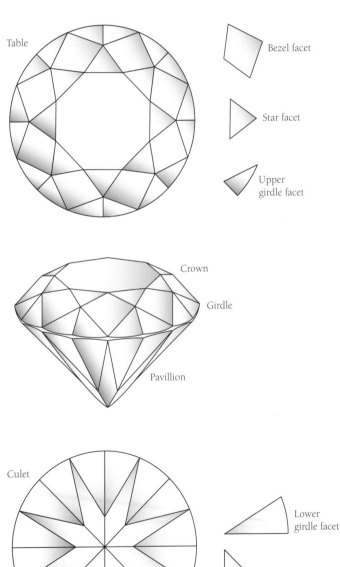

Translating Cut into Design

In the introduction, I told my story of becoming obsessed several years ago with an image of a gemstone and how I wanted to transform it into a quilt. I remember staring at that image for hours. I had no knowledge of the gem anatomy I just described (page 17). However, as my eyes scanned the light and color that tumbled across the image, I began to detect order within the chaos. Repeating shapes began to emerge.

First to emerge were the pie-shaped wedges radiating from the center. Once I recognized these wedges, I was able to pick out the kite shape that formed the narrow part of each pie-shaped wedge. Then I noticed that a quadrilateral balanced *en point* atop the kite. I really got excited when I realized that the side points of each quadrilateral met up with the side points of the adjacent quadrilateral—as if they were all holding hands and dancing around the edge of the gemstone.

I had just identified the crown facets of a round brilliant-cut diamond—the table, kite, star, and upper girdle facets. This was the key to the puzzle! I would piece the diamond using each facet as a separate "block" in my pattern.

If you apply this idea to an image of an up-facing brilliant-cut round gemstone, you can divide the design into 48 distinct sections. Each of the 8 pie-shaped wedges includes 6 subsections: the kite wedge of the table facet, 2 halves of the star facets touching the kite facet, the kite facet, and 2 halves of the upper girdle facets.

Once the major facets have been identified, you can then begin to further divide them into the shards of light that dance around the inside of the gem. Depending on the complexity of the quilt you want to create, you could divide a facet into multiple subsections to reflect lots of sparkle or you could

simply keep the facet as one piece. The facet lines and the lines delineating the shards of color and light in these gems are going to be your seamlines. Always ask this question: How would I piece this back together?

When I'm searching for gems to use as inspiration, I evaluate each candidate by asking the following questions:

1. How can I separate the gem into sections or "blocks"? I search for the major "through lines" that divide the stone into discernible sections. For example, round brilliant cuts can be easily divided into half, then quartered, then further segmented into eighths. Here is another example.

Finding facets and shards of light within
Photo by Geoffrey Watt (Mayer & Watt)

2. How can I reduce the number of Y-seams needed to piece this back together? *Y-seams* are created when 3 pieces of fabric come together, causing 3 different seams to converge at 1 point. Most gems will require some Y-seam piecing. For example, an emerald cut has 2 major Y-seams in the center of it.

If you don't want to tackle Y-seams, you can straighten the facet line and create a *y-seam* instead. By a *y-seam*, I am referring to seams where 3 pieces of fabric come together, but only 2 seams converge.

3. If there are multiple lines of the facets and shards of light converging in 1 place, can I offset them and still keep the integrity of the design? In most cases the answer is *yes*! In fact, I purposely offset seams in my gems for this very reason. And when you look at gems, you'll see light bouncing every which way; it's not lining up perfectly at the points. Light does *not* conform to quilters' rules!

The next challenges centered around construction. For example, how would I keep track of all the little templates once they were cut apart? Each piece would require its own unique identifier to indicate where it belonged within the gem.

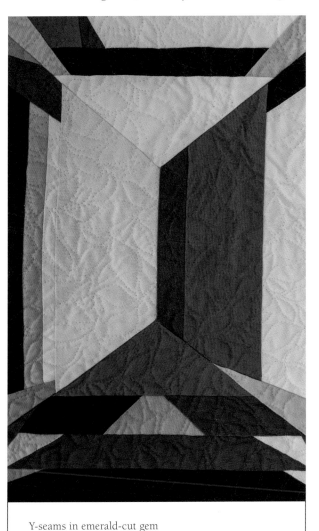

Y-seams in emerald-cut gem

Ametrine
Photo by Geoffrey Watt (Mayer & Watt)

Since I try to capture as much of the sparkle of a gem as I can in my quilts, I like to subdivide each facet into lots of little pieces. Some of my larger quilts have over 1,000 separate pieces, each with its own template.

I decided to code my early gems with a single unique number: 1, 2, 3 … 345, 346, 347, and so on. Then I learned the hard way that my mind tends to wander at about piece 300. I start skipping numbers.

That reminds me of the story about the high school seniors who released three little pigs into the school on Senior Prank Day. But before they did, they attached numbers to their collars: 1, 2, and 4. After retrieving sweet little Pig #1, Pig #2, and Pig #4, the staff spent the rest of the day searching for nonexistent Pig #3.

When I realized I was spending far too much time searching for "Pig #3" pieces—pieces that never existed in the first place—I decided to use a code comprised of two digits separated by a hyphen. The first digit represents the section number, while the second digit represents the unique piece within the section. For example, a piece coded "3-5" would be the fifth piece in Section 3. This reduced the potential for mistakes. We'll talk in more detail about planning your unique identifier codes in Chapter 3 (see Unique Identifier Codes, page 66).

Unique hyphenated identifier codes

Catching the Light: Fire and Brilliance in Gems

I'm a nut for color. While actual images of gemstones are the inspiration for my art quilts, I take great liberties when translating a gem's original color into my design. For example, I might take an image of a pale, yellow citrine and boost the color to a fiery red-orange, and then sprinkle complementary hues of purple and blue around the design as I did with *Devil's Due* (page 99).

When I work with students to create their own gem designs, the topic of color produces the most anxiety. With an entire rainbow of colors available to them, many students freeze at the prospect of picking five or six colors. While this book is not intended to be a treatise on color, here are a few tips that I hope will help restore the fun to selecting color for your gem.

Banded orange sapphire
Photo by Geoffrey Watt (Mayer & Watt)

DEFINITION OF TERMS

Let's start this discussion by defining a few terms that will help clarify some of the concepts. I'm going to use the words *color* and *hue* interchangeably. In color theory, a *hue* is a pure pigment—without any shade or tint (added black or white pigment, respectively). Hues are the pure colors that surround the edge of a color wheel and can be defined as red, orange, yellow, green, blue, purple, or a combination thereof.

Value, on the other hand, refers to a hue's lightness or darkness. You probably created a value chart in a middle school art class by adding different amounts of white paint to produce a progression of *tints* (lighter values of a hue), and conversely greater amounts of black paint to produce a progression of *shades* (darker values of a hue).

Himalaya mine bicolored tourmaline
Photo by Geoffrey Watt (Mayer & Watt)

Fire in Ice: Capturing Color (Hue)

There is no "perfect" color choice for a gem. Rubies, sapphires, emeralds, citrines, aquamarines, peridots, garnets, and all other lovely gemstones can be found in a wide variety of hues and shades. For example, all sapphires aren't blue. Some are pink, yellow, green, or even orange! Rubies can come in deep purple, bright red, or a soft pink. Emeralds range from dark green to a light celery color.

Beyond the inherent color of a gemstone, ambient light and environment can also impact the color you see. Alexandrites are famous for their "personality" change depending on the light in which they are viewed. In natural light, alexandrites may appear blue-green; in artificial light, they appear reddish-purple. Gem aficionados sometimes refer to alexandrites as "emerald by day, ruby by night."

Mixed fancy sapphires
Photo by Geoffrey Watt (Mayer & Watt)

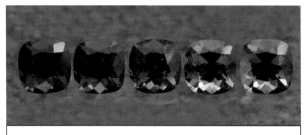

Spinels of various hues
Photo by Geoffrey Watt (Mayer & Watt)

Alexandrites in different lighting
Photo by Geoffrey Watt (Mayer & Watt)

D   H   N   Z

GIA D-Z color examples of the diamond grading scale
Photo by Gemological Institute of America (GIA)

White diamonds are prized for their *lack* of color. The most highly valued diamonds reflect pure white light without any tint at all. Those that show a faint yellow or gray tint are deemed lower in value—until the yellow crosses a threshold and becomes a rich hue, at which point it is classified as a *colored diamond*. More on colored diamonds to follow.

The flashes of color—blue, yellow, red, green, purple—you see in a spectacular white diamond are its *fire*. Fire is the result of light splitting into different color wavelengths before bursting out through the crown. (This is different from *brilliance*, which I'll discuss a bit later in this chapter.)

Let me throw one more curve at you. Heavenly objects known as *colored* diamonds exist. The gemological name for a colored diamond is a *fancy diamond*. Fancy diamonds are caused by an anomaly in their molecular structure.

For example, blue diamonds (such as the famous Hope Diamond) contain boron particles within their crystal structure. Green diamonds have had a few molecules knocked loose as a result of sitting too near an irradiated rock. Deep rich yellow and orange diamonds include nitrogen molecules that absorb blue light, causing them to throw off a yellow color.

Hope Diamond
Photo by Chip Clark, courtesy of the Smithsonian Institution

Fancy diamonds are categorized by the intensity of their hue. Gemologists use terms like "faint," "very light," "fancy light," "fancy intense," "fancy vivid," and "fancy deep" to describe diamonds of deepening hues.

Given that there is no "perfect" color for any gem, you can relax and let the fear go. This is *your* gemstone. Make it any color you want!

Lavender zoisite
Photo by Geoffrey Watt (Mayer & Watt)

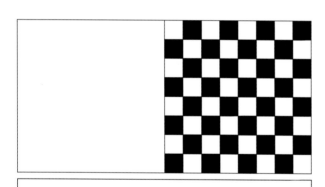

Demonstration of value contrast

Brilliance: The Role of Value Contrast

The interplay between different tints (lighter values of a hue) and shades (darker values of a hue) can bring drama to your work by creating stark delineations of form and spatial illusions.

The interplay between light and dark is of profound importance in the gem world. In the diamond industry, *brilliance* refers to the pure white light that is reflected back to your eyes through the crown of a diamond. It's the pop of light that captures our attention.

For a diamond to be at its most brilliant, though, it needs more than just brightness. It needs contrast. It needs the dark bits.

Imagine a blank sheet of white paper and a chessboard of alternating white and black squares. The sheet of paper returns twice the amount of light to our eye than the chessboard, but the chessboard appears brighter than the blank sheet. Why? The contrast between the black and the white further define and delineate their stark values.

You can use the idea of brilliance to make your work sparkle, no matter what type of quilts you make. If you want to bring out the bling in your work, *put the lightest lights and the darkest darks next to one another* and watch what happens.

Translating Color and Value Contrast into Design

I generally allow the image of a gem to guide my initial color choices. For example, *Between River & Sky* (page 104) was inspired by a lovely aquamarine and citrine cut by German gem cutters Wild & Petsch. I studied the image and identified a few basic hues within each.

Within the aquamarine, my eye primarily saw aqua (greenish blue), clear blue, and slate (grayish blue). While the hues of the citrine were in the yellow and yellow-orange range, I wanted a deeper, richer color palette for that stone in my quilt. As a result, I selected hues in the gold, orange, and red-orange family for the citrine.

Why did I place the aquamarine and citrine gems together? They have hues that are opposite one another on the color chart—complementary colors. Colors that sit opposite one another on the color wheel make each other pop and create lots of drama. Drama was what I was going for.

Because I like to add drama to my "diamond divas and drama queens," I often play with complementary colors. Earlier in this section I mentioned *Devil's Due* (page 99), in which I paired yellowish orange fabrics with purplish blue fabrics, perfect complementary colors.

I played up the color in a similar way with *Angel's Share* (page 99), creating the heart-shaped diamond in a variety of warm hues (yellow, gold, orange, and red-orange). Then I added a background of painted electric blue fabric. The result? A composition with lots of "zorch!" (You won't find that term in any dictionary: It was coined by a friend to describe the jolt you get when you see knockout color combinations.)

Fire & Ice (page 100) and *Old-Fashioned New* (page 100) are both built on the interplay of colors opposite (or close to opposite) on the color wheel. *Blush* (page 98) is built on a complementary palette of blue-greens and red-oranges.

Aquamarine
Photo by Wild & Petsch

Citrine
Photo by Wild & Petsch

Investing a few dollars in a good color wheel or color chart will go a long way to building your color confidence. You can find them in any art supply store. Some quilt shops carry them, too, so be sure to ask. C&T Publishing offers several quality color tools.

SO VERY GEORGIA O'KEEFFE

Do you know what Georgia O'Keefe is attributed to have said about complementary colors? Colors adjacent to one another on the color wheel are friends, while colors opposite one another are *lovers*. That's so Georgia!

You can use value contrast with dramatic results, too. For example, if you want to simulate the gradual deepening (or lightening) of a particular hue within a section, you can arrange a progression of values next to one another, creating a gradient effect or color wash. If, on the other hand, you want to highlight the sharp edge of a facet, place two fabrics of starkly different values next to one another.

An effective way to determine the color values of the fabrics you've selected is to use the grayscale filter on your phone. This is a helpful technique, especially when you're attempting to determine the value of two different hues.

Arrange your fabric from lightest to darkest as best you can. If you have an iPhone, you can look at the image through your phone application using a grayscale filter before you snap the picture. If you're using an Android phone, you must snap the picture first and then open it in your gallery application to apply the grayscale filter.

Look carefully at the grayscale image and ask yourself a few questions:

1. Are there one or more fabrics that are out of place in the progression of value? If so, move the out-of-place fabrics to their more suitable locations within the progression.

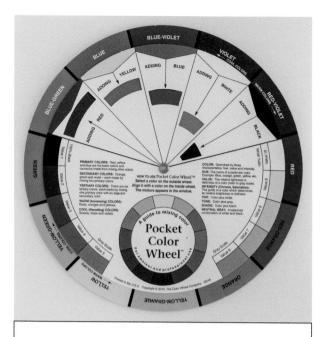

Color wheels are good investments.

2. Are there two or more fabrics that have about the same value? If so, consider removing one of them to simplify your choices.

3. Is there a stark difference in value between two fabrics that you've placed next to each other? If so, consider adding one or more fabrics of values that bridge the gap between the two.

Once you've adjusted the order, added fabrics, or subtracted fabrics, take another look through your grayscale filter and reassess. Do the fabrics flow evenly in value from one to the next? Are more adjustments needed?

Artist Josef Albers noted that very few people are able to distinguish value similarities between different hues. A bright pink fabric and a brilliant blue fabric appear to be of vastly different values. But when you evaluate them through a grayscale filter, they are virtually indistinguishable. If you're using two or more hues and you're struggling to combine them all into one value progression, try this technique. Separate the fabrics into piles by their common hue (that is, reds together, blues together, and so on). If you have two piles, arrange the fabrics in each pile in a value progression next to one another. Snap an image and compare them using the grayscale filter.

Using the same three questions (previous page), adjust each column of fabric so that the values flow evenly across the fabrics.

Now you can begin to merge the two columns into one. Lay like values next to one another. Even though they are different hues, they have the same value. You already know which ones are similar in value, so at this point you can start auditioning your fabric by removing fabric swatches, evaluating your reaction to the new combination.

Repeat with various fabric swatches, eliminating those that don't appeal to you, until you winnow the selection to a manageable number. Of course, the definition of manageable is up to you. Remember: I suggest using no more than one or two basic hues and only a few corresponding shades and tints of each.

You can also use any one of the gorgeous commercial gradation fabrics available in the marketplace to create a gradual flow of color across the surface of a facet.

Here are a few ways I like to use value contrast, particularly the concept of brilliance, in my work.

Effect 1: Shimmer

Imagine you're gazing out across a lake while the sun hovers over the horizon in front of you. See the millions of tiny sparkles shimmering on the water? The combination of the brilliant light and the deep shadows creates a mesmerizing effect.

By combining light and dark pieces in a symmetrical fashion through the surface of your quilt, you can add the same kind of shimmering brilliance to your work. This is a powerful effect that you can use in quilts that aren't intended to have a defined focal point. Many traditional block quilts fit this category.

While I usually spend time in my studio on my gem designs, I sometimes get the chance to put together an occasional traditional quilt. A few years ago, I made the pinwheel quilt shown here for a friend using clothing that belonged to her late father. I intentionally placed light and dark fabrics next to one another to create maximum sparkle across the top.

This pinwheel quilt uses value contrast to create a shimmering effect.
Photo by MJ Kinman

Effect 2: Traffic Lights

You can also use the placement of light and dark fabric to direct your viewer's eye across the quilt. These areas of light and dark act like traffic lights, helping your viewers visually navigate through your composition.

Pathways of lighter-colored areas invite your viewer's eye to move across them, while deep pools of darkness slow down your viewers' treks across the composition, giving them a chance to rest and rejuvenate. As a result, your quilt comes alive with movement.

Peach zoisite
Photo by Geoffrey Watt (Mayer & Watt)

Detail of *Char #4* (page 102)

As an example, I fell in love with the peach zoisite that inspired *Char #4* (page 102) precisely because of the river of light that flowed through its center. I wanted to be sure to capture that stream of light in my final design.

To replicate the river of light across the gem, I deliberately positioned areas of white and lighter-colored fabric across the central portion of the quilt. Then I surrounded them with areas of black and deep brown tones. As a result, your eye moves easily across the central part of the design.

A second example is *Devil's Due* (page 99). When I first pieced this quilt, I was not satisfied with the result. It looked flat and lifeless. Not only was it missing the brilliance I wanted to capture but it was also missing the focal point—the tip at the bottom edge of the quilt. It didn't have the punch I wanted.

Once I replaced a few of the long facets in the lower left part of the diamond with pure white fabric, it all came together. The splash of white added more sparkle, and the pathway of light moved the viewer's eye more effectively to the focal point. Her inner diva came through!

Detail of *Devil's Due* (page 99)
Photo by Cliff Patrie

Effect 3: Spotlight

A third way to use the idea of brilliance in your designs is to highlight one or more specific places on your quilt by packing them with the lightest lights and darkest darks. Areas of great contrast draw the eye to them and can create loads of drama in your work.

Lila (page 102) is inspired by the very first crystal that caught my attention. I loved the way the light dove into the top left of the solitaire and exploded out the bottom right facets. In my design, I created areas of pure white and light fabric to highlight those focal points and, to boost the brilliance, I placed fabric of darker values around them.

Lila

Rutilated quartz
Photo by Geoffrey Watt (Mayer & Watt)

Luminous Wonders: The Clarity of a Gem

While clarity is a concept typically associated with diamonds, clarity is a quality factor in all gemstones. *Clarity* describes the unique "birthmark" of a gem, either internal (called *inclusions*) or external (called *blemishes*).

Inclusions and Blemishes

Diamonds are formed deep within the earth under extreme heat and pressure, and they explode to the surface through volcanic action. It's no surprise that most diamonds bear some type of inclusion as a result of their dramatic creation stories.

Colored gemstones, too, are evaluated for their clarity. For example, sapphires and rubies often contain long, thin inclusions called *needles*. Emeralds typically contain inclusions that can be seen without a microscope. Emerald inclusions are often described as mossy or garden-like. In fact, sometimes they are referred to as *jardin*, French for "garden."

Blemishes are the external chips, nicks, or scratches that have resulted *after* the formation of the gem-stone. These normally occur during the cutting, mounting, or wearing of the gem.

Inclusions within a tricolored tourmaline
Photo by Geoffrey Watt (Mayer & Watt)

Translating Clarity into Design

The illusion of clarity in your gem quilt depends on your choices in surface design, which of course means the fabric you select. I've used solids, prints, batiks, hand-dyed fabric, and hand-painted fabric to create my gemstones.

SOLIDS

I made my first gem quilt with solid fabrics. You can't go wrong with the consistent, rich color that fabric companies are producing today. The downside of using solid fabrics is that you can't create the illusion of light floating up through the crystal (its translucence) like you can with gradient, hand-dyed, or hand-painted fabric. To create the impression of a gradual value change, you must piece several fabrics of similar value color together to achieve the gradation.

PRINTS

I experimented early on with prints and decided they were not my top choice for the visual impact I wanted to make. Prints are created to call attention to themselves. Since I want viewers of my quilts to look at the whole quilt, not the individual parts, I shy away from dramatic prints.

In addition, if you put different prints together, you can end up with a confusing mishmash of styles. This could distract from the coherent whole that you're striving for. If you mix stripes and florals and textured prints, it's like listening to a classical

Prints in *Roses for Sister Eilerman* (page 95)

symphony, country music, and zydeco on the same station. All those different genres, which are great all by themselves, are a little off-putting when played one right after the other.

You can minimize the impact of singling out individual pieces of the gem by using the same type of print for all the facets. This provides a consistent look across the design. However, it can be difficult to find the different colors of a single print to achieve the look you are going for.

GRADATIONS

Fabric companies have been creating gorgeous gradations for years. These work well in gem quilts when you're searching for fabric to provide a progression of lights to dark in one fabric swatch. Many gradations also display changes across the color spectrum, providing even more interesting opportunities.

However, you are limited to the prescribed length and span of the gradient. If your gem requires a long, subtle change from one value to the next, you'll have to piece it with solids rather than use a tight gradient.

BALI HAND-DYES

I can't tell you how much I love Bali hand-dyed fabrics. These were my go-to fabrics for many of my early quilts. The color values rippling across the surface resemble the cloudy interior of a gemstone. But they can be limiting when you're aiming for the appearance of a long, subtle wash of color or a perfectly clear pool of color.

Bali hand-dyes in *Nikki's Wedding Quilt* (page 96)

HAND-DYED FABRIC

Hand-dyed fabrics are delicious to find and fun to buy. If you decide to dye your own fabric, you'll need to make space in your studio to manage the chemical process. My home studio doesn't have the facilities to handle all the chemicals, rinsing, and drying needed to dye fabric, so I've stayed away from this option.

HAND-PAINTED FABRIC

My preferred method of creating the illusion of clarity in my quilts is to paint my own fabric. I use Jacquard Products' Dye-Na-Flow fabric paint. I love painting fabric, because in a process that is highly premeditated and precise, painting is wild, gestural, and spontaneous.

Sample of MJ's hand-painted fabric

Hand-dyed fabric in *Penumbra* (page 96)

Creating Light: Painting Fabric

I used solid fabrics for many years to create my gem quilts. I also experimented with prints, but I wasn't satisfied with the way they distracted from the overall design. Then I turned to batiks, hand-dyed fabrics, and gradations, but all had their limitations.

I reluctantly realized that I was going to have to paint my own fabric to get the effects I envisioned. Despite my hesitation, I bought supplies, dove in … and loved it! In stark contrast to the precise and premeditated process I use to design and code my quilts, painting fabric is wild, gestural, and provides immediate satisfaction. It results in some pretty amazing fabric, too.

Here are my suggestions if you'd like to experiment with fabric painting.

Photo by MJ Kinman

TOOLS AND MATERIALS

100% cotton sateen or prepared-for-dying (PFD) fabric, at least 44″ wide and pressed to remove major creases and wrinkles

42″ canvas stretcher bars: Set of 4 (available at art supply stores)

Staple gun and staples

Dye-Na-Flow fabric paints (by Jacquard Products)

2″- to 3″-wide paintbrushes: 2 or 3

Plastic bowls

Paper towels

Large tarp

Drop cloth

Plastic tablecloth or small tarp

Spray bottle filled with water

Vinyl gloves or other protective covering for your hands

Hairdryer

Steps to Create Hand-Painted Fabric

1. Assemble the stretcher bars by joining the ends at right angles. Place 2 staples spanning the mitered joints on both the front and back of the frame.

2. Place the frame on a table with the flat side of the stretcher bars facing up. Drape the pressed fabric loosely over the edges, making sure the shiny side of the sateen faces up.

3. On one side of the frame, staple the fabric onto the edge in 4 or 5 places.

4. Move to the opposite side of the frame, pull the fabric taut, and staple the fabric again in 4 or 5 places.

5. Repeat on the remaining sides. Finish up by stapling the corners.

6. Secure a large tarp against a wall so the top edge is at least a foot above the top edge of the frame. The tarp should drape down the wall and pool on the floor. The tarp will protect the walls and floor from splatters.

TIP
Curtain Rods Make Great Tarp Hangers

I installed curtain rods over my design wall and threaded clips onto them to hold the top edge of the tarp.

7. Place a drop cloth over the tarp that extends across the floor. This provides extra protection for the floor and prevents the frame from sliding.

8. Lean the frame against the wall with the tarp and on top of the drop cloth. The tarp on the back wall should not touch the back of the cotton sateen.

9. Cover the worktable where you'll stage your paints, bowls, and paintbrushes with the plastic tablecloth to protect from spills.

10. Fill plastic bowls with water for rinsing paintbrushes. Set several layers of paper towels nearby for drying paintbrushes.

11. Arrange paints on your worktable in the order in which you'll use them. I typically apply the lightest color first.

12. Wearing protective gloves, pour the first color of paint into an empty plastic bowl. A little paint goes a long way, so start with 5–6 teaspoons of paint in the bottom of the bowl. Recap the bottle to prevent spills.

13. Dip a paintbrush in the paint and, with the spray bottle in one hand and a brush in the other, apply the paint gently to the fabric in a broad sweep.

TIP
Avoiding Drips and Drops

Loading up the brush with lots of paint can result in unwanted drips. Instead, add small amounts of paint to the fabric in rapid succession. You should not slap the paint onto the surface. This may result in small drops of paint bouncing onto areas of unpainted fabric. If you do get drips, however, no need to fret. Blend these little inclusions into the overall design.

14. To achieve a gradual wash of color from medium to near white (resulting in a gradual brightening value study), feather the color across the fabric in short, overlapping vertical and horizontal strokes. As the color lightens, dip the brush into clean water to remove excess pigment and dab it onto the paper towel to remove the water. Use the spray bottle to mist as needed to push the color around the fabric and to facilitate blending. If drops of water create little areas devoid of color, continue to feather them out with the brush.

15. To achieve a gradual flow of one color to a different color, pour the first color into the bowl and apply it to the fabric. Replenish the original color in the bowl and add a tiny drop of the second color you want to achieve and mix. Apply the second color next to the original one and, using short horizontal and vertical strokes, blend the 2 together. Remove excess paint that the brush has picked up during this action before continuing to work on the wash. Continue to add more of the second color to the paint bowl, applying next to the worked fabric, feathering and blending as needed. To end with the second color, use it in full strength and blend.

 TIP
Saturation

It is difficult to achieve a deep black with this spray method because water dilutes all pigments. The best you can achieve is a dark gray. To achieve a pure black, apply the paint directly onto dry fabric or use a commercially available solid.

 TIP
Channeling Helen Frankenthaler

I prefer to stand while painting fabric because it gives me more control over the placement of the paint. (And it makes me feel a bit like Helen Frankenthaler, the amazing twentieth-century abstract painter.) If you prefer to paint the fabric while it is lying flat, raise the frame several inches above the work surface with blocks. If the frame is not raised high enough, the wet fabric will sag and touch the surface below. This will hamper the flow of paint across the surface and result in uneven paint application, striping, or dense spots of color.

Photo by MJ Kinman

CHAPTER 2

Set the Stage: Creating Gorgeous Compositions

Now that we've discussed some of the basics about how to piece together your gem, select colors, and audition fabric to give the illusion of clarity, let's spend some time talking about composition.

Detail of *Between River & Sky* (page 104)
Photo by Tony Bennett Photography

Tools and Techniques

I want to introduce you to some powerful online tools that can help you create your dramatic composition. These online tools, in addition to some old-fashioned physical manipulation of images, are how I create the mock-ups for most of my gem quilt designs.

You can find dozens of free image-editing applications by searching the internet. These applications download to your computer and connect with your picture files. They provide a work space where you can manipulate your original images to enhance them or create a new image altogether.

Of course, you can also pay for sophisticated image-editing software, such as Adobe Photoshop. That might be a perfect choice for you if you are preparing to publish your images. However, I find that often the more advanced apps like this require considerable time and effort to learn. Many other apps—*free* apps—don't have the steep learning curve and still give you the power to improve, transform, and otherwise modify your original images.

(Disclaimer: Most of my "play time" is spent using Photoscape, a free app. However, when I'm ready to create artwork for my patterns or other publications, I use my subscription to Adobe Illustrator and Adobe InDesign to do the heavy lifting.)

I'd like to introduce you to some of the image editing functions I use the most. There are many more functions included in these apps, and I encourage you to explore them. The ones I describe, however, will get you started down the path to awesome design. I'm using a gorgeous sunstone gem from the collection of Mayer & Watt to demonstrate the next few ideas.

1. First, let me assure you that these apps typically have an Undo or Reset button that will restore your image to its original state. You can audition certain looks for your gem and then easily clear them if it's not the look you're going for.

2. Remember to save your modified image with a new filename once you have created the look you want. This will allow you to preserve your original image in case you want to use it again in the future.

Platinum zoisite
Photo by Geoffrey Watt (Mayer & Watt)

Yellow-green sunstone
Photo by Geoffrey Watt (Mayer & Watt)

Color and Value Modifiers

All image-editing apps will allow you to modify the color and value of your image. Here are the four functions that I use most often.

Hue

This function changes the hue (color) of your original image. By sliding the toggle bar up and down the continuum, you can change the hue of the original image from, say, blue to green, yellow, orange, red, purple, and back to blue.

Change image color using image-editing apps.

Saturation

The saturation tool allows you to increase or decrease the amount of gray tones in your image. By increasing the saturation you remove gray, producing an image with purer hues and more vibrancy. Conversely, reducing the saturation adds more gray tones, resulting in a softer, more muted image. Take the level of saturation all the way to zero, and you end up with a nearly perfect gray scale of your image.

Intensify image color using image-editing apps.

Intensify value contrast using image-editing apps.

Contrast

The contrast tool enhances or dulls the light and dark areas. By boosting the contrast, you brighten the light areas and darken the shadows. By reducing the contrast, the lights and darks mellow into a range of gray tones without much distinction between them. The image becomes misty, as though a veil of fog has rolled over it.

Remove color and assess gray scale using image-editing apps.

Gray Scale

Image-editing apps typically allow you to view your image in gray scale. In Chapter 1, I described how to put together a selection of fabrics with a good progression of values (light to dark). Once you have selected your fabric, matching those values with the gray scale of your gemstone will help you tremendously in assigning fabric color to the facets in your gem.

Preset Filters

Most image-editing apps have a series of preset filters that allow you to easily achieve a specific effect without having to fiddle with the individual hue, saturation, and contrast settings. If you open up the filter tool, most display modifications of your original image in thumbnail images so that you can compare and select just the filter you want.

Using Color and Value Modifiers in Design

When I was preparing to launch the first pattern of my Diamond Divas series, I designed *Elizabeth* in a blue colorway inspired by a lovely light-blue princess-cut diamond. However, I wanted to offer *Elizabeth* in additional colorways, including pink and yellow.

Instead of trying to find images of gemstones with the alternate color palettes I envisioned, I decided to play with the original image of the first *Elizabeth* in an image-editing app to create the pink, yellow, and neutral palettes myself.

Once I opened Photoscape on my computer and selected the original image of *Elizabeth*, I used the hue setting to alter the image from blue to red. Next, I tweaked the saturation and contrast settings until I found an image I liked. I repeated the exercise with the yellow colorway.

Three options for *Elizabeth* pink colorway

Elizabeth from the Diamond Divas pattern series

Peach zoisite
Photo by Geoffrey Watt (Mayer & Watt)

When I began searching for a gem to use for a new Bourbon Diamond design, I looked for a fiery gem-stone with a red-orange glow. I remembered that I had once seen a gorgeous, pale peach zoisite in the online collection of friends Laurie and Simon Watt, international gem dealers.

I loved everything about the little oval gem—its shape, its color, and especially the river of light that swept across its surface. I wondered what it might look like if I modified the color in an image-editing app.

Modified peach zoisite image

I loaded the image to Picassa, which has a preset filter called Boost. This filter increased the image's saturation and contrast. When I clicked on the filter, the little zoisite caught fire! I knew immediately that was the inspiration for my *Char #4* (page 102).

Directional Modifiers

Tilt

Image-editing apps allow you to tilt an image to the left or the right. In some instances, you may decide to align an offset gem to an imaginary horizon. In other instances, you may want to tilt an image to create energy in your design.

Some apps provide a toggle bar that tilts the image to the left or the right, while others allow you to input a numeric value identifying the degree of tilt that you desire. Entering a positive number such as 25 will tilt your image 25° to the right; a negative number such as -25 will tilt your image 25° to the left.

Using tilt function

Flip

Let's say you found the perfect image for your next project, but it's pointing the wrong direction. Image-editing apps have a solution for that. You can create a mirror image of your gemstone on either the vertical or the horizontal axis. In other words, if your image faces left, you can flip it to face right by selecting the vertical flip function. If it's pointing up, you can flip it to point down simply by using the horizontal flip function.

Using flip function to flip right to left

Using flip function to flip down to up

Rotate

You may simply want to change the direction of your image by a clean 90°, 180°, or 270°. The rotation function allows you to spin an image either clockwise or counterclockwise by one-quarter of a full circle.

Using Directional Modifiers in Design

After I had landed on the fiery color for my little zoisite, I played with the alignment functions to see how I responded to the image at different angles. I tilted it, rotated it, and flipped it vertically and horizontally. I settled on a 45° tilt clockwise, which placed the river of light flowing diagonally from the top right of the stone to the bottom left.

Gem rotated 90° clockwise

Crop Function

Image-editing apps also allow you to remove unnecessary parts of an image with the crop function. This tool allows you to zoom in on interesting areas and delete the part of the image outside the boundaries you've selected.

Using crop function

Using the Crop Function in Design

Once I had changed the zoisite's color and direction, I cropped the image to preserve just the upper portion of the gemstone, including the river of light flowing through it. I dropped the "ceiling" of the cropping square to cut a slight bit from the top of the gem. This created a pair of wonderful negative spaces to the left and right of the tilted gem, delineated by the sexy curve of the gemstone. I had my final design!

Final mock-up of *Char #4*
Photo by MJ Kinman

Tips for Creating Great Compositions

Now that you've mastered some of the features of image-editing apps, you can use them to create exciting designs. My early gem quilts were simple portraits of gems. They were placed in the center with all edges visible within the frame of the quilt. I positioned the gems in this way because I wanted to prove that I could capture the essence of a gem. I felt that including the entirety of the stone was the best way to do that.

However, a few years into the adventure, I decided to make quilts that were a bit more sophisticated in their composition. I had no idea what that might look like or how to do it, but with experimentation, my design process evolved. This is by no means a treatise on composition, but I hope it will provide a jumping-off point for you.

Fascinate with Focal Points

Simply by placing your focal point in different areas of your design, you can create all kinds of moods. If you want to create a design that conveys gravitas, solidity, and permanence, consider placing the focal point or main feature of your design in the very center of your quilt.

However, if you want your design to exude energy and motion, consider placing the focal point of your design off-center using the rule of thirds.

The Rule of Thirds

The *rule of thirds* suggests that the most visually powerful placement of your subject is along imaginary grid lines that segment your design space into thirds both horizontally and vertically—or at their intersecting points.

Fancy zoisite
Photo by Geoffrey Watt (Mayer & Watt)

Energize with Angles

I once heard an artist say that if you want to add kinetic energy to your work, place your subject in a position that isn't sustainable over time. In other words, knock your subject off balance. That's where you'll find your energetic point. *Char #4* (page 102) is a perfect example of knocking my subject off balance. The gem looks like it's toppling to the left.

In another instance, I experimented with the juxtaposition of sapphire blue and fiery orange facets for *Old-Fashioned New* (page 100), separating them with a horizontal line. Even though the line was positioned in line with the rule of thirds, it just didn't have the energy I wanted.

As I played with the frame surrounding the blue and orange facets, I tilted it to one side, transforming the horizontal line into a dramatic angle rising from left to right. I knocked it off balance. The resulting angle added energy to the composition.

Between River & Sky (page 104) was designed with several strategies in mind. I wanted this piece to have the gravitas of a medallion quilt but with a hint of rebelliousness. While the citrine superimposed on the aquamarine is set in clean horizontal and vertical planes, the gem is placed just off-center. I shoved it a little bit to the upper right of the design to create visual interest and a subtle energy.

Entice with Off-Page Placement

My earlier gems were portraits of the full stone. You could see the outside edge of the entire gemstone within the quilt. In later quilts, however, I cropped the gem down to its most interesting features. For example, *Devil's Due* (page 99) is inspired by a cushion-cut diamond, a four-cornered gem with gently rounded sides. I knew I wanted one of those four corners to be the focal point of the composition, so I tilted the image about 45° and cropped everything out except the lower half of the gem.

Dos and Don'ts When Using Gems as Inspiration

1. Do look for a gem with personality. I search for gemstones that either have a unique color, shape, cut, or all of the above. Using the techniques I described, you can modify a gem's original features to make it more interesting, as I did with the peach zoisite that inspired *Char #4* (page 102).

2. Do keep in mind the question "How would I piece this back together?" as you study the facets of a gem. If the gem has many facets converging in one spot, can you design it so that the seams are offset?

3. Do consider looking for multiple gems to include in your design. Consider placing more than one gem in the same composition. They could be the same type in terms of shape, color, and cut, or they could have contrasting shape and color. The three voluptuous cushion-cut gems that inspired *Communion* (page 97) had the same basic shape and cut but were of contrasting colors. The two gems that inspired *Blush* (page 98), were dramatically different sizes and contrasting colors. I loved bringing these two stones together to create drama.

Padparadscha sapphire
Photo by Geoffrey Watt (Mayer & Watt)

4. Do experiment with modifying the image (boosting color, cropping, rotating).

5. Don't let your background detract from the focal point. In the first two compositions of the Angle of Repose series, *Communion* (page 97) and *Blush* (page 98), I added embellishment to the negative space between the gems. In hindsight, I didn't need to do that. I feel now that the juxtaposition of the gems creates a strong enough composition.

6. Do keep notes about your progress so that if you need to take break for a period of time you can reengage with your work without having to take too much time playing catch-up.

7. Don't attempt to copy the image exactly. This image is a slice of the infinite ways that gem reflects light. Further, you don't want to run afoul of copyright laws or permissions. If you're using specific

gems from a collection, ask permission from the owners if you can. I have written permission from my gem-dealer friends to use any gem in their collection as inspiration. I cite them and the photographer when writing about them and showing images of the original stone.

8. Don't try to use an actual gemstone as your image source. It will drive you crazy. The color and brilliance of your gem will change with the tiniest movement of the gem or light source. If you want to create a portrait of a beloved gem and you don't have a photograph to guide you, here's how to go about it. First, determine its cut. Find a drawing of the cut online and study the facets. Find an image online of a gem that resembles your gem in shape, cut, and color. Create a composition inspired by your research. Voilà! A portrait of your beloved gem.

PART II

CREATING YOUR GEM QUILT

CHAPTER 3
Creating a "Star Chart": Freezer-Paper Piecing Techniques

Congratulations! You have discovered an amazing gem that inspires you and created a composition that delights your heart. Now you're ready to transform your design into a quilt using the powerful technique I've been using for over twenty years to make my own giant gem quilts: freezer-paper piecing.

I'll walk you through each step of creating a mock-up of your design and transferring it to a full-size freezer-paper pattern. My husband refers to these patterns as my "star charts," because he thinks they look like constellation maps. I love that analogy. I think that is an apt term to describe the patterns for our own divas, too! These patterns will help bring your own stars to life.

Not only will you learn about each step of the process in this chapter, you'll have the chance to practice them, too. I have created a small gem quilt project for you to work on as we move through each step of the process. After the description of each step, we'll apply it to the sample project so you can put the concepts into practice. The sample project, *Lovely Laurie*, is inspired by a beautiful Mozambique purple garnet from the collection of Mayer & Watt (as photographed by Geoffrey Watt).

You'll find the Mozambique Purple Garnet design mock-ups in the appendix (page 109).

Mozambique purple garnet
Photo by Geoffrey Watt (Mayer & Watt)

Overview

1. Create a mock-up of your final design using an appropriate ratio between mock-up and final quilt.

2. Trace the major facet lines on the mock-up.

3. Draw horizontal and vertical grid lines on the mock-up. The width between your grid lines is determined by the ratio between the mock-up and the final freezer paper you select.

4. Assemble the full-size freezer paper using double-sided tape to join the edges of the paper together.

5. Draw horizontal and vertical grid lines on the freezer paper with an erasable pencil. The width of your grid lines is determined by the ratio between the mock-up and the final freezer paper you select.

6. Draw major facet lines on the freezer-paper chart using a ballpoint pen or other permanent writing tool. Consult the mock-up to determine line placement.

7. Erase the horizontal and vertical grid lines on the freezer-paper chart.

8. Draw lines inside each major facet on your freezer-paper chart to replicate the shards of light and color, using your mock-up as your guide.

9. Identify the hues and progressive values of your design and assign each an alphanumeric code.

10. Select fabrics that correspond with each color code.

11. Create a color key that includes the alphanumeric code and a snippet of its corresponding fabric taped or pinned next to it.

12. Assign a color code to each shard on your freezer-paper chart using an erasable pencil (in case you wish to make changes later.)

13. Assign a unique identifier code to each shard within each major facet on your freezer-paper chart.

14. Place hash marks in a random manner on each line segment on your freezer-paper chart. Use a different color pencil or pen.

15. Make a copy of the freezer-paper chart using your home printer or a large-format printer at a copy shop or reprographic shop. (*Reprographics* is a blanket term encompassing multiple methods of reproducing content, such as scanning , photography, xerography, and digital printing. I use it, however, to refer to shops that specialize in copying very large images, such as architectural blueprints. Reprographic shops often charge far less for a large-format print than a regular copy shop.)

16. Reassemble the freezer-paper chart with double-sided tape as needed. Assemble the paper copy if necessary and place it next to your work area.

17. Assemble business-size envelopes or plastic baggies, and write a color code on each one.

18. Cut up your freezer-paper chart with a rotary cutter and ruler.

19. Sort freezer-paper pieces into envelopes or baggies by color code.

Introduction to Sample Project: Mozambique Purple Garnet

Finished block: 18″ × 18″

This beautiful Mozambique purple garnet from the collection of Mayer & Watt inspires our sample project. I love her marvelous purple and pink hue, as well as the great value contrast across her facets. The hexagon cut will be fun to piece, too. I've completed the first three steps of the process for you.

I've created the mock-up, which you will find in the appendix (page 109).

I've traced all the facet lines, as well as the interior cuts of light.

I've added the horizontal and vertical grid lines.

At the end of each step, I'll walk you through the decisions I made as I selected and created the mock-up. When we get to the point of assembling the freezer paper, selecting colors, and coding the star chart, you'll get to do all those steps right along with me. The directions that I provide result in an 18″ block that you can use to make a mini-quilt or pillow.

SAMPLE PROJECT TOOLS

Freezer paper: 18″ wide or precut sheets, either brown or white color (Freezer paper is a paper product used by butchers and crafters. It is available in 15″ and 18″ widths and as precut sheets. It is also available in some areas in brown and white colors. One side of freezer paper appears as a regular paper surface that you can write on; the other side is coated with a waxy substance. This waxy coating is what allows it to adhere to fabric without leaving a residue. Please note that freezer paper is *not* the same thing as wax paper or parchment paper.)

Regular erasable pencil

Colored pencil in a light color: Light green, pink, or blue

Eraser

Fine-tip ink pen or permanent marker

Double-sided tape

18″ ruler and smaller 6″ or 9″ ruler, each with ¼″ measurement

Highlighter pen (for example, yellow or pink)

Hand-held correction tape dispenser, like Bic Wite-Out EZ Correct (*Do not use liquid correction fluid.*)

Rotary cutter (2 cutters if you prefer using a different rotary cutter for paper and fabric)

Rotary mat

Home printer for copying final freezer-paper template (*Or take freezer-paper template to a local copy or reprographic shop.*)

Business-size envelopes or plastic baggies: 6

Iron

Basic sewing supplies (scissors, pins, seam ripper)

Tweezers

Fabric marking pencil(s) to mark on dark and light fabric

Basic sewing machine

SAMPLE PROJECT FABRICS

I noted the Painter's Palette Solids from Paintbrush Studio Fabrics that I used below. A fat eighth measures 9″ × 20″–22″ and a fat quarter measures 18″ × 20″–22″.

White: Fat eighth or ⅛ yard (PPS 121-000 White)

Light pink: Fat eighth or ⅛ yard (PPS 121-018 Petal)

Light dusty pink: Fat quarter or ¼ yard (PPS 121-024 Orchid)

Medium dusty pink: Fat quarter or ¼ yard (PPS 121-152 Clematis)

Medium purple: Fat quarter or ¼ yard (PPS 121-027 Purple)

Dark purple: Fat eighth or ⅛ yard (PPS 121-080 Amethyst)

Black: ½ yard (PPS 121-004 Ebony)

Backing and binding: 1 yard (for 18″ × 18″ quilt)

Batting: 22″ × 22″

Create a Mock-Up

Your design is beautiful! You're pleased with the composition and can't wait to transform it into a quilt. The next step is to create a small mock-up of your final design. This step is mandatory if you're going to transfer the design to freezer paper using the grid technique described in detail below. However, creating a mock-up is valuable even if you're going to use a digital projector to project the image directly onto the freezer-paper template.

Plan the Mock-Up

I find that I get the best results when I print out a mock-up of my design (a close approximation to the appearance of my final quilt). In the mock-up, I need to be able to identify the facets that will serve as my blocks and trace their outlines with a pen or pencil. In addition, the mock-up must also help me identify the shards of light and color that intersect each facet.

How large should the mock-up be? Since I print out my mock-ups on my ink jet printer, they can be no larger than the narrowest margins of an 8½″ × 11″ sheet of paper.

I typically create mock-ups that have a ratio to my final quilt of one inch (1″) to one foot (1′). In other words, if I want my final piece to be 6′ wide and 4′ tall, my mock-up must be 6″ wide and 4″ tall.

However, your work may be smaller than mine, and so a 1″ (mock-up) to 1′ (freezer paper) ratio may result in a mock-up that's just too small to be useful. For example, if you are planning your final quilt to be 3′ wide and 4′ tall, a 3″ × 4″ mock-up might be too small to capture the details of the facets and light that you'll need to create your larger piece. Try creating a mock-up that is twice that size: 6″ × 8″. Your ratio would then be 1″ (mock-up) to 6″ (freezer paper).

In general, I coach students through the process of creating a mock-up plan in a way that doesn't get them too side-tracked by the math.

Use these guidelines for good results:

- Plan the width of your mock-up to be a whole number: 4″, 6″, or 8″.

- Divide your mock-up into a number of segments that is easily divisible by the total *width* of the design. Remember: You can always divide your mock-up into 1″ segments for easy planning.

A few examples:

- If your mock-up is 4″ wide, divide it into 2 columns that are 2″ wide.

- If your mock-up is 6″ wide, divide it into 3 columns that are 2″ wide.

- If your mock-up is 8″ wide, divide it into 4 columns that are 2″ wide.

- Draw vertical lines onto your mock-up the desired width apart (based on your choice above).

- Now draw horizontal lines onto your mock-up the exact same desired width apart (based on your choice above). It's okay if you have partial columns at the bottom; we'll calculate that into the size of your freezer-paper chart.

- Determine the width of your final quilt.

- Divide that width of your quilt by the number of columns that you chose for your mock-up. Example: If you segmented your mock-up into 4 columns, divide the width of your quilt by 4. That calculation will be the width of your grid lines, both vertical and horizontal.

- If the final width of the quilt will be 4′ and you divided the mock-up into 4 columns, the width of the freezer-paper grid lines will be 1′. (4 ÷ 4 = 1)

- If the final width of the quilt will be 5′ and you divided the mock-up into 4 columns, the width of the freezer-paper grid lines will be 1¼′. (5 ÷ 4 = 1.25)

- If the final width of the quilt will be 6′ and you divided the mock-up into 4 columns, the width of the freezer-paper grid lines will be 1½′. (6 ÷ 4 = 1.5)

Your mock-up could be as simple as a printout of the gem(s) you wish to use in your design pasted onto construction paper and cut to the desired size. This is how I created the mock-up for many of my giant gems.

You can also create a mock-up using a graphic design application like Adobe Illustrator (which requires a monthly subscription) or a free online version like Canva.com. These apps allow you to select the size of your starting "canvas" so that you can print it out to the desired size. The power of these apps is that they allow you to upload images and use them to create a composition. They also allow you to add background color, line, and shape elements to your design.

Project: Create a Mock-Up

I have created the mock-up that will serve as your guide for the final quilt (see the appendix, page 109). You can use the 6″ × 6″ mock-up to create any-size quilt you wish. Whether it be 6″, 18″, 48″, or even larger, we'll discuss how to convert the mock-up to the quilt size you want.

The composition of our mock-up is straightforward. It's a portrait of our beautiful Mozambique purple garnet, with all the edges within the boundaries of the quilt. The six-wedge design is familiar to many quiltmakers, and the straight seamlines make for easy piecing.

Trace the Facet Lines onto the Mock-Up

Once you've printed out the mock-up, take a pencil and trace the outlines of your major facets.

1. For example, if your inspiration is a round brilliant cut, search first for the kite facets. Find at least one and extrapolate from that one. Your gem might not have per-fectly delineated facets. Draw them in where you think they belong. Remember, that if your gem image is tilted in any way, the top points of the kite facet might be beyond the gem edge. That's fine!

2. Once all your kite facets are holding hands around the circle, connect their "toes," the points that face toward the center of the gem. You now have identified your table, star, kite, and upper girdle facets.

3. Look deep into the table facet and decide how you're going to piece it together. Find—or create—one major line that divides the table facet into 2 halves. If you feel those 2 facets are manageable as separate sections, you can leave it at that. If, however, the 2 table facets will end up having more facets than you care to track, further divide each half by finding the lines that run through it.

Sometimes you need to take some artistic liberties with the shards of light and color to corral them into a quilt pattern. Don't be shy or hesitant about it—this is *your* diamond. There is no right or wrong answer. Have fun!

Keep in mind the importance of offsetting your facet lines just a bit to prevent converging seams. Your eye "sees" what it wants to see. My first solitaire had 12 seams converging at the central point. It was a mess! I quickly learned that I could offset the seams at any one point. Again, light doesn't follow quilters' rules!

I generally trace only the major facet lines on my mock-up. If I were to trace all the lines delineating the color and light shards, my mock-up would get way too busy and overwhelm me. The main purpose here is to help you identify the major blocks. We'll deal with the smaller pieces on the freezer paper.

Project: Trace the Facet Lines onto the Mock-Up

While I typically trace the facet outlines of my mock-up with a regular pencil or pen, for this particular mock-up, I used Adobe Illustrator to draw the facet lines onto the image. I wanted to do this to show how you can modify the lines from the original gem (see the appendix, page 109).

Instead of drawing our mock-up to include all the facets within this lovely gem, I decided to take some artistic liberties. I offset a few of the lines separating the light and color to make it easier to piece, and I did not delineate every single change in color and value—best to keep our first project together relatively simple.

The final mock-up is one that I believe will reflect the loveliness of the original gem and yet result in a quilt block that will be fun to piece and will delight your eyes.

Sample project facets

Draw Grid Lines on the Mock-Up

Now you're ready to place your grid lines over top of your facet lines. Using a different color pencil, trace the lines that will create the number of columns and rows that you determined earlier.

Why a different color? With all these lines and color shooting through your mock-up, it can get pretty confusing trying to figure out which are facet lines and which are grid lines. Using a different-color grid line provides a visual clue that it is indeed a grid line that you're looking at and not a facet line. This becomes critically important as you begin to replicate the facet lines on the freezer paper.

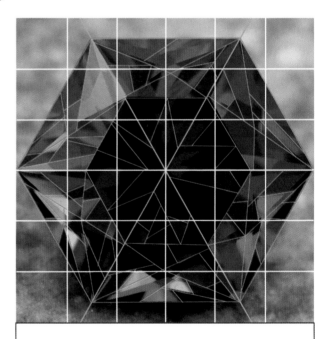

Use light pencil to trace grid lines on mock-up.

Project: Draw Grid Lines on the Mock-Up

I used Adobe Illustrator to draw light yellow grid lines in 1″ intervals over the mock-up. Always keep an eye out for the possibility that a grid line might overlay a facet line. In this case, the central horizontal line of our mock-up is obscured by the central horizontal grid line (see the appendix, page 109).

Create a Full-Size Freezer-Paper Chart

Assemble the Freezer-Paper Chart

You're now ready to prepare your freezer-paper chart. Cut lengths of freezer paper to size according to the final dimensions of your quilt. Freezer paper comes in rolls that are 15″ and 18″ wide and in precut 8½″ × 11″ sheets. I typically use the 18″ width.

Place double-sided tape on the edge of one length of freezer paper. Carefully overlap the tape with the back of the edge of a second length of freezer paper. Be careful to keep the edges of the freezer paper sheet parallel. If you used 2 pieces of freezer paper 18″ wide, you now have a sheet that is approximately 35″ wide. (The 2 freezer-paper sheets 18″ wide overlap by about ½″, reducing the total width of the combined 36″ by approximately 1″.)

Repeat with additional freezer paper until you have created a sheet *the full size of your final quilt dimensions.*

TIP
Use Precut Freezer Paper

C&T Publishing offers Quilter's Freezer Paper Sheets as an alternative to commercially available rolls. The 8½″ × 11″ sheets work well with our sample project. You will need a total of 6 sheets for the Mozambique Purple Garnet project.

1. Place double-sided tape on the non-waxy side of the sheet's lower 8½″ edge.

2. Carefully overlap the upper edge of another sheet of freezer paper to cover the double-stick tape. (The regular paper side of each freezer-paper piece should be right side up.)

3. Repeat to create 2 more pairs of freezer-paper sheets.

4. Place double-sided tape on the long edge of 1 pair of freezer-paper sheets.

5. Carefully overlap the long edge of another pair to cover the double-stick tape. (The regular paper side of each pair of freezer-paper sheets should be right side up.)

6. Add the third pair of freezer paper sheets to the first 2 using double-stick tape.

7. Draw an 18″ × 18″ square on your joined freezer-paper sheets.

8. Once you've completed your chart codes, gently pull apart the freezer paper to reveal the double-stick tape.

9. To make a copy of your chart, place each separated 8½″ × 11″ sheet facedown on your home printer and select *Copy.*

10. Once all copies have been made, reattach the freezer-paper sheets and the regular paper copies with double-stick tape according to your original design.

Project: Assemble the Freezer-Paper Chart

Using 18″-wide freezer paper, cut an 18″ length from the roll. We're going to use a ratio of 1″ to 3″ to enlarge our 6″ square mock-up to an 18″ block. This fits perfectly with an 18″ freezer-paper length, though you can also use precut sheets of freezer paper (see Tip: Use Precut Freezer Paper, page 55).

Using a Digital Projector

I purchased a digital projector a few years ago to project images of my mock-ups directly onto freezer paper. I have found that the enlarged images are blurry, and the color isn't as true as I would like. In the instances when I've used the digital projector, I've always printed out the mock-up and referred to it throughout the process. Then why use a digital projector? It simply saves you the step of tracing the grid lines onto your mock-up and your freezer paper.

When using a digital projector, be mindful of cords. You don't want to hurt yourself or your projector by tripping over cords and sending your projector crashing to the floor. I recommend taping the cords to the floor to keep them in place and reduce tripping hazards.

Using the Grid Technique

The grid technique forces me to truly study my design and make changes to the design on the fly if I need to. But I suppose the real reason I enjoy this technique is that I love maps. This is simply a mapping technique that allows me to lay down the lines of my gemstones using the coordinates created by the horizontal and vertical grid lines.

TIP
On or Off the Wall?

Because my freezer-paper charts tend to be large, they are unwieldy to produce on a tabletop. As a result, I prefer to tape my large freezer-paper template to my design wall before adding the grid lines and facet lines. A 4′ carpenter's bubble level helps to draw perfectly horizontal and vertical grid lines.

You may prefer to work with more manageable-sized freezer-paper charts, so you would more likely be able to add grid lines and facet lines working on a table surface.

Using an erasable pencil, lightly draw horizontal and vertical lines in the desired widths on your freezer-paper template. Draw on the side that looks like regular paper—the side you can easily write on. Do not draw on the waxy side. The waxy side will be facedown on your fabric. Why use an erasable pencil? Because once you've drawn your facet lines over the grid lines, you'll erase the grid lines to reduce the visual noise on your freezer-paper chart.

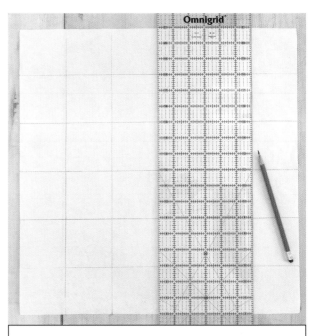

Add grid lines to freezer-paper chart with erasable pencil.

Transpose the Major Facet Lines of Your Design to the Freezer-Paper Chart

Using a *non-erasable* pen or marker, transpose the major facet lines of your mock-up onto the freezer paper.

If you're using a digital projector to project your mock-up on the freezer-paper chart, adjust the size of the projected image by moving the projector closer or further away from the wall until the image fits the freezer paper. Adjust the focus until the image is sharp. Be sure to tape the projector power cord to the floor or otherwise protect it so that you don't stumble over it as you trace the facet lines of your image.

I recommend having a physical copy of your mock-up available to you during this process. The image projected on the wall can be fuzzy in areas and a physical mock-up will help clarify line placement. This printed mock-up will also be helpful when you start adding color codes to your freezer-paper chart.

 TIP
Use Non-Erasable Pen or Marker to Draw Facet Lines

You must use a non-erasable pen or marker to draw facet lines, because in a few minutes you'll be erasing those light pencil grid lines. You don't want to damage your lovely facet lines as you're getting rid of the grid lines!

If you're using the grid technique, use the horizontal and vertical grid lines as reference points to determine where to place your facet lines on the freezer-paper chart.

1. To get started, take a look at your mock-up. Find the major "through line" of your design—the one line that splits your design into 2 parts—if you have one. Otherwise, select a kite/bezel facet to start with.

2. Once you've identified the first line, you'll transpose that line to the freezer-paper chart. Find its origination point on the freezer-paper chart grid. Where is it located in reference to the closest grid lines?

In our *Mozambique Purple Garnet* project, the first through line on my mock-up is the horizontal line that splits the image into perfect halves. That's pretty easy to spot and transpose to the freezer paper.

So, let's look for the next through line. I'm going to use the intersecting line that originates at the top left of the design, intersects the design at the dead center, and terminates at the lower right edge of the design.

How would you describe the origination point of this line? It appears to be about one-third of the way across the top of the second column. Next, I'll find the corresponding point on my freezer-paper chart, about one-third of the way across the second column from the left. I'll place a mark there with my ballpoint pen or permanent marker. (By the way, what is ⅓ of 3″? 1″! If you want to measure 1″ to place your mark, feel free. But you can certainly eyeball the placement of your mark for now. We can adjust later.)

3. Now look for the line's termination point on the mock-up. Where is it located to the closest grid lines? In this example, the termination point on the mock-up appears to be about two-thirds of the way across the fifth column. So, I'm going to find the corresponding position on my freezer-paper chart—about two-thirds of the way across—and make a mark with my pen or marker. (Again, what's ⅔ of 3″? 2″! If you want to measure, feel free. Once more, it's okay to eyeball the placement of the termination mark.)

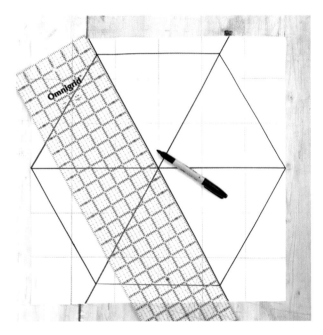

4. Now let's see where that line intersects the grid lines on the mock-up. In this case the line intersects the exact center of our design. So, I'm going to go back to my freezer paper and connect my origin and termination points with a straight edge or ruler. Does the edge of the ruler intersect the exact center of the freezer-paper grid lines? If not, simply adjust your ruler so that the line runs through the intersecting grid lines at the dead center of your design. Are you happy with it? Once you're satisfied with that line, use a pen or permanent marker to scribe the line on the freezer paper.

Continue using this process of using the start and end points of lines on your mock-up to estimate and scribe lines in your freezer-paper chart. Again, keep in mind that you can offset your facet lines if you want to prevent lots of seams from converging

at one point. I'll say it again: Light does not conform to quilters' rules! You can move those little lines any which way you want. This is *your* gemstone.

TIP
Modifying Lines Already Drawn

If you decide to change a facet line on your freezer paper, you can easily do this by covering it up with correction tape. Hand-held correction-tape dispensers are a wonderful invention. I used to eliminate unwanted lines by placing squiggle marks through them, but this ended up with lots of visual noise on my freezer-paper chart. Correction tape solves this problem. And you can iron over correction tape. On the other hand, please don't use correction fluid. It will ruin your iron.

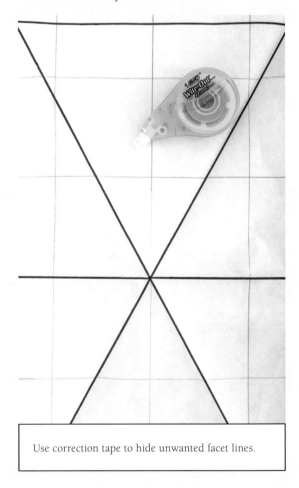

Use correction tape to hide unwanted facet lines.

5. Once all your major facet lines have been drawn on your freezer paper, erase those lightly penciled grid lines.

Project: Transpose the Major Facet Lines to the Freezer-Paper Chart

1. Using an erasable pencil, lightly draw lines 3″ apart horizontally and vertically on your freezer-paper template.

2. Use non-erasable pen or marker to draw facet lines.

- Find the major through line of your design on your mock-up. The through line is the line that splits your design into 2 parts. In our case, it is the center horizontal line that splits the design in perfect halves.

- Draw the first line on the freezer-paper chart. This one is going to be easy because it follows exactly the center horizontal grid line (the third horizontal line from the top.) Take your ruler and pen (or permanent marker) and draw a line over the center horizontal grid line.

- Find a through line that splits the top half of your mock-up into 2 sections. This isn't so easy, is it? That's because there are no lines within our lovely hexagon-shaped Mozambique purple garnet that split the top and bottom halves into 2 sections. So we get to create them!

  Since I like the energy of angled lines, I'm going to create a couple of through lines by extending the central intersecting facet lines all the way to the upper and lower edges of the mock-up. This will create 6 sections that can be easily coded and pieced.

- Transfer intersecting lines to the freezer paper. Clearly both lines intersect the exact center of the mock-up. All we need to do is find the origination

and termination point of each line. And this is all just guesswork—nothing scientific about it.

Let's look for the origination point of the line that extends from the top left to the lower right on your mock-up. It originates at the top of the mock-up near the halfway point of the second column from the left—but not quite.

On the top edge of your freezer-paper chart, locate the halfway point of the second column from the left and then move your pen slightly to the left. Make a mark.

Now drop your ruler onto the freezer paper so that it aligns with the mark you just made and also runs right through the center point of your grid. Does the termination point look like it lands on your freezer paper at about the same place as it does on the mock-up?

If not, pivot the ruler slightly, keeping it aligned with the center point of your grid, and draw your line. See how easy that is? It's *your* gem. That line can be any angle you want it to be.

Do the same thing with the intersecting line that runs from the top right to the lower left. Drop a mark where you think the line originates. Drop a ruler so that it aligns with both your mark and the center point of the grid. Do you like where it lands at the bottom of your freezer paper? If not, pivot the ruler, keeping it on the center point of the grid, and draw your line.

Voilà! You have 6 major sections that you can now begin to slice into pieces.

- Draw the edges of the garnet on your freezer-paper template. Take a look at the horizontal line at the top of the mock-up between the 2 intersecting section lines. It's about halfway between the grid lines of the top row. (Actually, it might be slightly closer to the top edge than the first grid line.)

Math whizzes might be inclined to measure the actual distance of the line between the upper and lower edge of the column, and to multiply the measurement by 3. This will give you the precise point to place your horizontal line on the freezer paper. If that gives you goosebumps, do it! But for us non-math geeks, remember: Precision isn't a priority with these gems! I dropped my line in the illustration about halfway between the top and the first grid line. And it will be *perfect*.

Do the same with the horizontal line at the bottom of the mock-up between the 2 intersecting section lines. Draw your line with your permanent pen.

Now that you've located the top and bottom edge of the gem, simply connect the dots to get the remaining 4 edges.

- Highlight the edges of the major sections and the outside edges of your freezer paper with a colored highlighter. This is another visual clue to help you know which edges should be placed along the grainline to help prevent stretching during the sewing process.

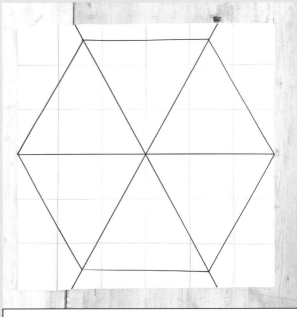

Draw major facet lines on project freezer-paper chart using mock-up as your guide.

Capture the Light Within the Facets on the Freezer-Paper Chart

With the outlines of your major facets now scribed on your freezer paper and with the grid lines gone, you can now start to carve up the interior of those facets with shards of color.

Working with one section at a time, segment the facet according to the shapes you see within your mock-up. I like to work with a magnifying lens close by so that I can dive deeper into the facet.

Here are a few pointers to keep in mind when segmenting the interior of the facets:

- Keep it simple on your first attempt. Don't worry about capturing every tiny shard and angle of the light. Instead, focus on capturing the major changes in color and value. You may see several colors that are close in value; feel free to combine those into 1 large piece.

- Pay attention to changes in value contrast. Capturing the darkest darks and the lightest lights will pay visual dividends. When you divide a section that will eventually become a light or white area, make a small notation in it (for example, "white" or "very light") This will be a great help when you go back over the facet to assign color codes.

- Change Y-seams to y-seams. If you see several shapes of color and light coming together that would result in a Y-seam, change it into a Y-seam. No need to make this more complicated than it needs to be. No one will know that you made the change as they're looking at your gorgeous gem.

- Offset your seams. If you see several facet lines colliding together in one spot, offset the lines. Again, there's no need to make piecing more difficult than it needs to be. Light bounces around gems in a million different ways and, once more, light doesn't conform to quilters' rules.

- Mix it up with different shapes and sizes. I like to see lots of contrast in my work, whether it is in color, shapes, or piece sizes. When you have a large piece surrounded by smaller pieces, it makes for a more interesting composition.

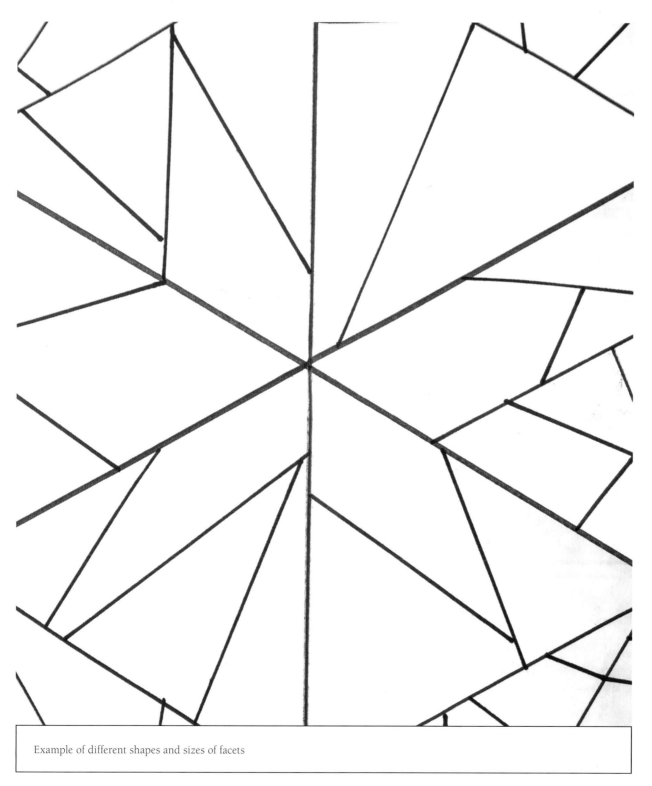

Example of different shapes and sizes of facets

- Forget about symmetry. You're going to get sick of me saying this: Light doesn't conform to quilters' rules! Light rarely obeys the laws of symmetry either. Some students ask me if they need to have the same number of pieces in each facet. No! Your mock-up is your guide. In some cases, an entire facet might be a single piece of fabric. This often happens when you find a gem that is reflecting oblique light off of an entire plane of a facet. Perfectly normal—and gorgeous!

- Manage washes of color. In some cases, you will see the boundaries of colors clearly defined in your gem. But in some pieces, you'll see a gradual wash of color. How you handle these washes within a single shard of light is partly dependent on the type of fabric you plan to use.

If you have decided to use solid fabrics, you can create the illusion of a wash by segmenting the large piece into smaller pieces and assigning color codes in a gradual value progression. If you have selected fabric that includes gradations of color—such as commercially available gradients, hand-dyed fabric, or hand-painted fabric—you can create the illusion of a wash by keep the piece whole and using a special color-coding technique I describe in the next section.

Project: Capture the Light Within the Facets on the Freezer-Paper Chart

What a gorgeous hexagon you've got there! You're now ready to draw the lines that make up the interior angles of light and color within each facet.

Working wedge-shaped section by wedge-shaped section, transpose the lines on the mock-up to your freezer paper. Use the same techniques you used to estimate the origination and termination points of the major facet lines. I obviously didn't follow the actual lines of the original Mozambique purple garnet to create our mock-up. Therefore, you don't have to follow mine. This is *your* gem! (You're going to get sick of me saying that, aren't you?)

Feel free to subtract lines from the design to simplify *or* add lines for more of a challenge. However, remember that more divisions mean smaller pieces. If you can handle small template pieces fairly easily *and* you are a confident piecer, slice it up! However, if this is your first attempt at freezer-paper piecing, you might want to stick with my design or even leave some of the lines out.

If you draw a line and realize it should have been placed elsewhere, use your correction tape to cover up the line.

Here is what your freezer-paper chart could look like. Label the top of the freezer-paper chart. Erase the grid lines from your freezer-paper chart.

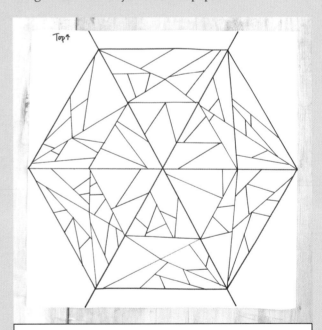

Shards of light and color within sample project

Coding the Freezer-Paper Chart

The coding system I describe here is all about providing you with visual clues that you can use to sew these little pieces back together. Imagine every piece of a 1,000-piece jigsaw puzzle dumped onto the table. That's what your freezer-paper templates are going to look like sitting on your work surface after you've cut them out of fabric: shards of light and color tumbling across the table. Most people will look at that amazing pile of color and wonder, "How in the world am I going to put these back together in exactly the right order?" You, on the other hand, will smile confidently and know you've got this. You know the codes.

Each piece you've drawn on your freezer-paper chart will receive 2 codes and a set of registration marks called hash marks. The first code describes its color. The second is its unique identifier, providing clues about its position in the entire gem. The third set of marks help guide your piecing as you sew each set together.

I typically use a letter followed by a numeric modifier for the color code (for example, Y1, Y2, and Y3 for light, medium, and dark values of yellow), while the unique identifier is always made up of 2 digits separated by a hyphen (for example, 1-15, 1-16, and 1-17). The reason one code is a letter and the other code is a number is to distinguish one from the other. If both codes were numerical, my head might explode when looking at the chart. The potential for error skyrockets.

Color Codes

I prefer to work on the color codes first before assigning unique numerical identifier codes. Determining how color flows across the facet is subject of interpretation and therefore change. As a result, I routinely add or subtract pieces from a facet after reviewing the color distribution of the mock-up a second or third time. If I wanted to make changes to color assignments after already completing the numbering sequence, I could very well end up with a hot mess. And I have.

I described the process of selecting fabrics to create your color palette in Chapter 1 (page 15). I'll review some of those pointers here and weave them into the larger task of creating a color key and assigning color codes to each piece in the gem.

1. Study the mock-up (or original gem image) to identify one or more basic hues found in the gem. (Remember: Hue is a basic color identity such as blue, red, yellow, green, and combinations thereof. They are the colors that ring the outside of a color wheel.)

2. Select the basic hues present in your gem. Keep it simple and start with a single hue for your first project.

3. Identify the range of tints or shades of your basic hue(s) in your mock-up or original gem image. Let's keep it simple for the first project. Try to identify no more than 2 tints and 2 shades surrounding your basic hue. These 5 values, along with pure white and black, will give you a strong palette to work with. With 5 values in 1 hue, can you see how complex the coding could become if you decided to work with 3 or more hues? With 3 hues, you could easily have 15 colors to choose from, plus black and white. That can result in option anxiety, and ultimately, frustration and paralysis.

4. Assign codes to each of your values. I use a letter to signify the hue and modify it with a number based on its value. For example, if I were working on an emerald and selecting an array of green values, I would use the letter "G." In my world, the lightest value always receives the modifier "1" while the darkest values receive higher numbers. Thus, I might create a set of codes that look like this:

G1 = Pale green (light celery)	G5 = Deepest green (deep forest)
G2 = Light green (mint)	
G3 = Medium green (kelly)	W = White
G4 = Dark green (leaf)	BLK = Black

When assigning letters to your color codes, be careful to use unique letters for each hue. This is why I use BLK to signify black. If I'm working with a sapphire and have a range of blue fabrics, I want to be sure

I can distinguish between the facets coded for blue and those coded for black. Both colors start with *B*.

In my early work, and in some cases in my patterns today, I use a unique letter of the alphabet for a specific swatch (A, B, C, D, and the like). This is a very helpful coding solution when I am creating a pattern in multiple colorways. For example, I created *Elizabeth* (the first of my Diamond Divas series) in blue, pink, yellow, and neutral. I could print 1 copy of the pattern using the alphabetical system rather than recoding everything in B1, B2, B3, and so forth for the blue colorway, and then create an entirely different pattern coded for R1, R2, R3, and so on for the reddish-pink colorway.

In the long run, choose the coding system that works best for the way your brain works!

5. Select color swatches to coordinate with your codes. If you've already placed your fabric in a value progression, it will be easy to accomplish.

6. Create a color key by writing the codes on a sheet of paper. Cut a small snippet of fabric from your swatches and, using double-sided tape, pins, or glue, secure the snippet of fabric next to its code. I also write the name of the project and the date on the top of the paper for the record.

7. Using an erasable pencil (in case you want to make different design choices later), assign color codes to your pieces, starting with the white and black pieces first. Work through one facet at a time in a systematic fashion.

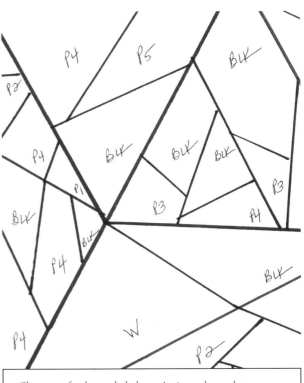

Close-up of color-coded chart. Assign color code to each piece.

Once you're confident that all the white and black pieces have been coded, select the next lightest color code and work your way through the design, identifying each piece.

After the lightest light is completely coded, move to the darkest dark color code. After awhile, you may notice that your white and lightest light pieces are right next to your black and darkest dark pieces. This is what gives your gem its brilliance!

Continue working through your color values until all pieces are coded.

TIP
Coding for Sweeps of Color

You may be working with a gem that has a flow of color across a single piece. If you have decided to use a gradient fabric or a hand-painted or hand-dyed fabric, decide on the range of codes that you see in the fabric swatch. Attach snippets of this area of the fabric to your paper color key. When coding the piece that contains the sweep of color, place several color codes that correspond with the gradient and connect them with a squiggly arrow. This is my visual clue to myself that I'm dealing with a color wash.

Commercially available gradient fabrics limit how you can translate the sweep of color in a gem to the striation in the fabric. You have far more flexibility if you decide to hand-paint your own fabric (see Creating Light: Painting Fabric, page 34).

Project: Add Color Codes to the Freezer-Paper Chart

1. Identify the hues and values of your design and assign each an alphanumeric code. After studying the Mozambique purple garnet, I saw purple and light red (pink) hues.

2. Select fabrics that correspond with each color code. I dove into my stash of Painter's Palette Solids by Paintbrush Studio Fabrics and began auditioning fabric. I selected a medium purple hue for my base color. I found my lighter values in stacks of pink and dusty pink swatches. The darker value was a single shade called Amethyst. I used the letter P for my main color code. See the sample project fabrics (previous page).

W —White	P4—Medium purple
P1—Light pink	P5—Dark purple
P2—Light dusty pink	BLK—Black
P3—Medium dusty pink	

3. Create a color key (see the bottom left photo on the previous page) that includes the alphanumeric code and a snippet of its corresponding fabric taped or pinned next to it.

4. Assign a color code to each shard on your freezer-paper chart using an erasable pencil (in case you wish to make changes later). Here's an example of what your chart might look like.

Unique Identifier Codes

The second code on each piece of your facets is its unique identifier. Each facet in your design should have its own unique code identifying its place in the design. No two should be the same. Think of it as the piece's address within the gem. The strategic placement of these codes will also help you piece the facets back together exactly where they need to be.

I described the unique identifier coding system in Chapter 1. It involves 2 digits separated by a hyphen. Here are steps and suggestions for successfully coding your gem's facets and pieces within those facets.

1. Identify the number of major facets in your gem. Assign each a section number. This is the first number in your 2-digit code. Working one facet at a time, label every piece in that facet with the first numeral and a hyphen following it. I like to use a different color pen to further differentiate between the codes.

2. Once you have coded each piece in a facet with its section number and hyphen, start at one side of the facet and begin adding the second digit: 1-1, 1-2, 1-3, 1-4, and so on.

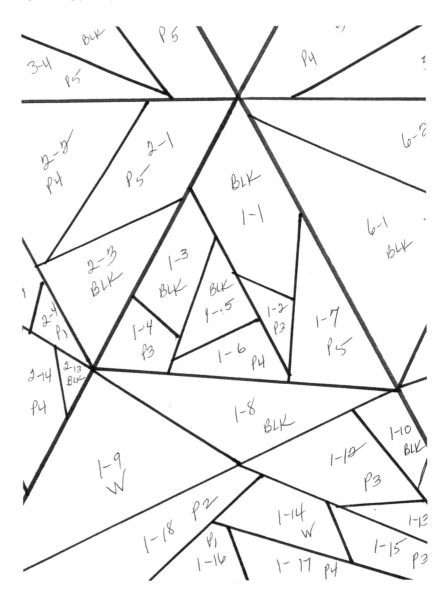

When numbering facets, it's important to keep your piecing strategy in mind. This is what I like to call the "Piece Plan." You are going to be sewing these pieces back together in units. Place adjacent numbers next to one another. If, however, you want to be sure to signal that you'll be starting a new set of units—meaning you won't sew one piece to an existing pair—consider placing that code a distance away from the last one in the series. Look at the example below. This numbering system provides another visual clue that you are putting the right pieces together. If you reach for a new piece to sew to an existing set and its code is out of order, you are more likely to say "Aha! These two aren't supposed to be sewn together right now. Let me find the right ones!"

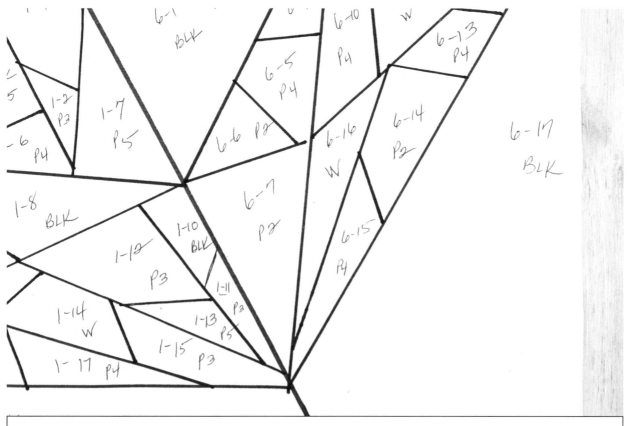

Consecutively number pieces to be sewn together as 1 unit. Adjacent pieces that will not be sewn together should not be consecutively numbered.

3. Review your codes to ensure that you haven't skipped a number. Remember the story of Pig #3 in Chapter 1!

4. If you find that you have indeed skipped a piece, no worries! You don't need to erase all your codes and start over. If you are splitting the piece coded as "2-3", add a lowercase *a* behind the "2-3". Label the additional piece "2-3b."

 **TIP**
Tricky Codes

When all your freezer-paper pieces are cut apart, it's very easy to mistake a piece coded "1-11" with a piece coded "11-1". To prevent confusion, put a line under these particularly tricky codes. The same can occur with pieces coded "9-6" and "6-9".

Project: Add Unique Identifier Codes to the Freezer-Paper Chart

Assign a unique identifier code to each shard within each major facet on your freezer-paper chart. Here's an example of how your freezer-paper chart could be coded.

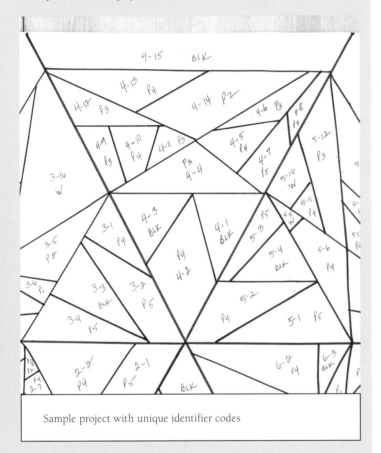

Sample project with unique identifier codes

Hash Marks

Hash marks are the little slash marks that cross the facet (seam) lines of your pattern. You will come to love these little guys because they are confidence builders. They provide visual clues that confirm you are indeed piecing the correct 2 freezer-paper templates together, and they warn you when you're not. Here are the important things to know about your new friends, the hash marks.

1. Consider drawing your hash marks using a colored pen that is radically different from the color you used to draw your seamlines. I use red or green. Why? After a while of drawing hash marks, I start to get distracted and skip areas. I've actually skipped an entire facet. How could I tell? There were gaps in the sea of green hash marks across my chart—yet another visual clue that my work wasn't quite complete.

2. Place at least 1 hash mark on the segment of a line between 2 intersecting seamlines. If you can fit in 2 hash marks, do it.

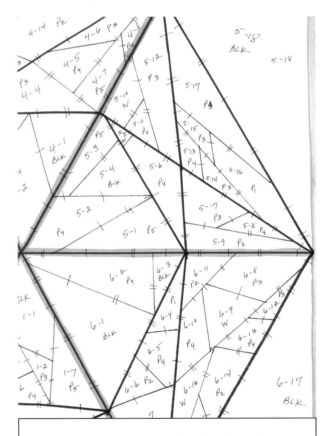

Each line segment must have at least 1 hash mark.

3. Draw hash marks as perpendicular to the facet line as possible.

4. Be sure that the hash mark extends all the way across the facet line and extends into the piece on both sides of the line.

5. Start this process by selecting one of the long lines between your major facets. Work along the entire length of the line from its start to the end. Each place you see another facet line intersect the line you're working on, that's the start of a new segment; drop a hash mark or 2 there.

6. Don't skip over tiny little line segments. These are the most important! Drop a tiny hash mark between 2 tight intersecting points, and you will thank yourself when the time comes to sew these pieces together.

7. Distribute hash marks as randomly across the line segments as possible. You don't want to automatically aim for the dead center of every line segment. For example, in one segment, place the hash mark one-third of the way between the 2 points; on the next segment, place the hash mark two-thirds of the way across the segment.

8. Randomize the number of hash marks in a set. Mix up the hash marks you draw, randomly alternating between 1 mark and a set of 2—or maybe 3—marks.

Why the emphasis on randomness? You will be sewing sets of freezer-paper templates together that have wonky shapes. There's nothing about them that screams, "We belong together!" It's easy to pick up 2 pieces that lie next to one another, but which should not be sewn together at that precise moment? You need a signal that you've picked up 2 pieces that don't go together! Hash marks holler at you to stop if this is what you're trying to do.

If you are holding 2 pieces that do indeed go together, the only thing that will match will be the seamline they share. And since you've drawn a hash mark—or 2 or 3—across that seamline they share, you will essentially be reuniting them. If the hash marks line up perfectly, you have a joyful reunion! That's why you want to drop them across the seam-line as randomly as possible; they will shout at you even louder if they don't match up.

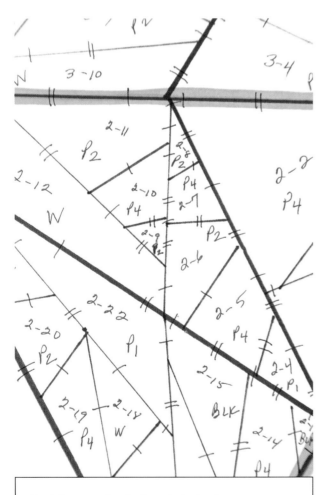

Don't forget to place hash marks in tiny line segments.

Project: Add Hash Marks to the Freezer-Paper Chart

Place hash marks in a random manner on each line segment on your freezer-paper chart. Use a different color pencil or pen. Here's what the hash marks on your sample project could look like.

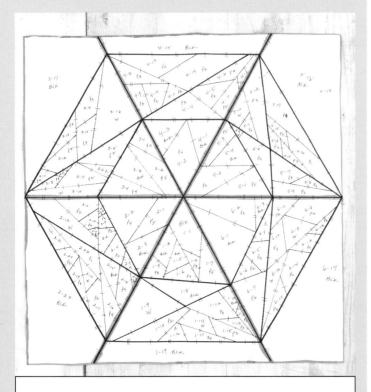

Hash marks on sample project

Copy the Freezer-Paper Chart

Congratulations—your star chart is complete! You have diligently placed all the visual clues you need to put this thing back together once it has been cut up. You're almost ready to cut up the freezer paper into all its tiny little shards of light and color … but not quite.

Before you pick up your rotary cutter and ruler, you *must* make a full-size photocopy of the chart. No "ifs," "ands," or "buts." This is a nonnegotiable step. You would never try to put a 1,000-piece puzzle together without the top of the puzzle box sitting next to you, would you? It would be a time-consuming, frustrating, and nearly impossible task. Same goes with trying to put together your freezer-paper templates without a paper copy to guide you. It would be a joyless undertaking.

If your chart is no larger than 8½″ × 11″, you can easily make a photocopy or scan your document and print out the results. If your chart is too big to fit onto the scanner bed, try folding it into even sections. Scan each section and name the file with a unique filename (such as Emerald 1, Emerald 2, Emerald 3, and so on). Print out the results and tape the sections together.

Since my charts are typically 5′ or more on any one side, scanning them on my home printer doesn't work for me. Instead, I use the self-service large-format printer at my local copy or reprographic store.

Large-format printers can print images up to 36″ in width and an unlimited length. They typically have 2 widths of paper rolls to choose from: 24″ and 36″. Copies are priced by the square foot. Therefore, if your chart is under 2′ in width, be sure to center the original between the 24″ marks to get the best pricing.

If your chart is under 36″ on the shortest side, you can run the entire chart through the printer without any preparation. If the shortest side is wider than 36″, here are the steps to prepare your chart for printing on a large-format printer:

1. Separate your chart into strips no wider than 36″ by gently separating the double-taped edges. If you used 18″- or 15″-wide freezer paper, you can run 2 taped lengths through the printer. (2 lengths of 18″-wide freezer paper that has been overlapped by ½″ with double-stick tape measures 35″ in width—perfect to run through the bed of the printer.)

2. Cut ½″ strips of regular paper and lay them over the exposed double-stick tape to eliminate its stickiness.

3. Roll up your freezer paper and take to the copy store or reprographic center.

If you haven't used a large format printer before, you'll be happy to know they have developed them to be as easy to use as regular self-serve printers. Most now require you to use a credit card to get started.

When you're identifying your print settings, be sure to always select the black-and-white option. Color copies are expensive.

Once you've printed out your copies, roll them up and head back home. At home, realign the sections of your freezer paper and secure them together with brand new double-stick tape. Use double-stick tape to secure the sections of your new paper copy. Hang it up on your design wall or close to your sewing table for easy reference.

Project: Make a Copy of the Freezer-Paper Chart

You can either fold your freezer-paper chart in half to fit onto your home printer or print at your local copy or reprographic shop.

Cut Apart the Freezer-Paper Chart and Sort the Pieces by Color Codes

You have successfully completed all your charting and are ready to start cutting! You are probably feeling a bit more relaxed knowing that you're headed back into your comfort zone where you can use beloved tools like rotary cutters, rulers, and eventually your trusty sewing machine. This is always a joyful transition point for me, too.

1. Manage your environment by closing any open windows and turning off any ceiling fans. Any source of a breeze across your table must be eliminated. You won't believe how easy it is for these little facets to disappear into cracks and crevices!

2. Gather business-size envelopes. The number of envelopes should be equal to the number of facet/sections *or* the number of different colors in your color key, whichever is greater. Write the color code on the upper left corner of the front of the envelope, as well as on the upper left edge of the back flap. (This makes it

easy to spot the correct envelopes regardless of whether they are laying faceup or facedown.)

3. With a rotary cutter, ruler, and mat, slice apart your chart along the major facet lines. Working one facet/section at a time, slice up the pieces along your seam-lines. While it's okay if you don't cut exactly on the line you've scribed, it is important that your cut be straight and not curved or wavy. That's why I use a rotary cutter and a nonslip ruler rather than hand scissors to cut apart my freezer paper.

If you have Y-seams in your design, be mindful of not cutting too far beyond the point at which the Y-seams intersect.

4. Once you've finished cutting up a facet/section, take a moment to separate the pieces into piles by color code. Then insert the piles into their respective color-coded envelopes. It's okay to fold freezer-paper pieces in order to fit them into the envelope.

Project: Cut Apart the Freezer-Paper Chart and Sort the Pieces by Color Codes

Working one section at a time, cut up your freezer-paper chart and sort into piles by color. Insert pieces in each pile into their respective envelopes.

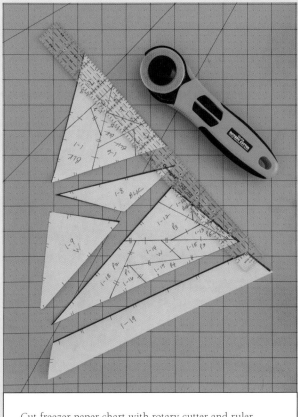

Cut freezer-paper chart with rotary cutter and ruler.

Sort pieces by color code.

CHAPTER 4

The Making of a Diva: Construction

Now we're safely back in our comfort zone, where we'll use familiar tools and techniques to assemble the quilt top. Below is a ten-step overview of the assembly process covered in this chapter. In this chapter, I'll also show you how to navigate special situations such as Y-seams, curves, multiple seams converging in the center, and needle-nose facets.

Overview

1. Iron the freezer-paper facets to the *right* side of the fabric based on color code.

2. Cut out the freezer-paper facets with a ¼″ seam allowance.

3. Sort the fabric facets by section code.

4. Working on one section at a time, arrange the fabric facets in piecing order.

5. Position pairs of fabric facets together using the hash marks to ensure alignment.

6. Sew the fabric facets together with a seam allowance that is a needle-width shy of ¼″ to avoid catching the freezer paper.

7. Press seams to the side. This allows the facet to lay flat on top. If there is no difference, press to the side of the darkest fabric.

8. After piecing an entire section, extend the hash marks of the facets on the edge of the section into the seam allowance with a fabric pencil before removing the freezer paper.

9. Repeat until all sections are complete.

10. Sew the sections together.

Position the Freezer-Paper Pieces Using the Color Code as Your Guide

1. Working with one color of fabric at a time, place the freezer-paper facets assigned to that color code on the *right* side of the fabric with the waxy side down.

2. Position the largest freezer-paper facets first, and place the smaller freezer-paper facets between them. Leave a generous ½″ gap between the edges of the freezer-paper facets so you can cut them out with an accurate ¼″ seam allowance. Use a hot iron, without steam, to adhere the freezer-paper facets to the fabric.

Consider grainlines when working with freezer-paper facets that have long edges or have edges bordering the quilt or a major section—whichever edge is the longest. If a facet lies along the outside edge of a major section, I place the outside edge of that facet along the straight of grain (the grain that is parallel to the selvage edge) to prevent stretching. You'll recognize these edge facets by the highlighted line you marked during the charting process. Placing freezer-paper facets along the straight of grain ensures stability during the piecing process.

The exception to this rule is for freezer-paper facets that contain multiple color codes. Multiple color codes on a freezer-paper facet indicate it should be positioned across several hues or values regardless of grainline. In my view, capturing the flow of light and color across the gem is more important than paying attention to grainlines.

3. Take one last look in your color-coded envelope or plastic baggie to make sure it's completely empty before you start to cut out your freezer-paper facets. Static electricity can cause freezer-paper facets to stick to the inside of the envelope and to one another.

Position edges of long facets and edges bordering sections on the straight of grain.

 TIP
When Facets Won't Stay Put

If the freezer-paper facet isn't adhering to the fabric, try this: Remove the freezer-paper facet, heat the fabric with a hot iron (no steam), then iron the freezer-paper facet to the heated fabric.

WHAT TO DO WHEN A FACET COMES UP MISSING

I've certainly lost my share of freezer-paper facets over the years. If you find that one is missing, here are a few things you can do:

- Check your envelope or baggie again. That little freezer-paper facet might be stuck to the inside.

- Check the back side (waxy side) of the larger pieces. Static electricity can cause freezer-paper facets to stick together.

- If you've already ironed your freezer-paper facets to the fabric, check for evidence that you may have inadvertently ironed a smaller piece between the larger facet and the fabric. It will appear as a lighter area under the larger freezer-paper facet.

- Check your fabric to make sure you've cut out all the freezer-paper facets. Some of them might still be ironed to the fabric. Those little ones are easy to overlook.

- Check other section envelopes for the missing freezer-paper facet. You may have accidentally sorted it into the wrong section pile.

- Check around your cutting table, including the base plate of your iron. Sometimes little facets get stuck between the metal base plate and the body of your iron.

- If you still can't find it, use your paper key to trace a copy of the missing facet onto a spare piece of freezer paper. Be sure to add the hash marks and codes on the replacement freezer-paper facet.

- If you don't have spare freezer paper lying around, take one of your larger facets and center it over the missing piece on the paper key. Trace the shape into the body of the larger freezer paper piece, being sure to add the hash marks and codes, too. Cut the missing piece from the larger facet. This will result in a hole in your larger facet, but that won't make a bit of difference in the end result.

Cut Out the Freezer-Paper Pieces

1. Before you start cutting out your fabric facets, write the major section numbers on the envelopes you previously used to sort facets by color. (I reuse my envelopes from one project to another. They are covered in crossed-out color and section codes!) (Remember: Section numbers are the first number in the unique identifier code.) As you cut out your fabric facets, drop them into the envelope with the correct section number.

If you prefer to cut out all your fabric facets before sorting them, use a box or basket to hold the fabric facets so that they don't wander away during the cutting process. You can sort the fabric facets into piles by section number later and then tuck each pile into its respective envelope or baggie.

2. Use a rotary cutter and a ruler to carefully cut out the fabric facets with a precise ¼″ seam allowance. *This is the one aspect in the process where accuracy matters.* Snip the ends of the needle-nose facets to within a ¼″ of the tip. This will help reduce bulk on the back of your quilt during piecing.

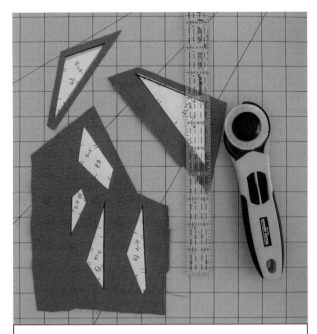

Use ruler and rotary cutter for straight, precise ¼″ seam allowances.

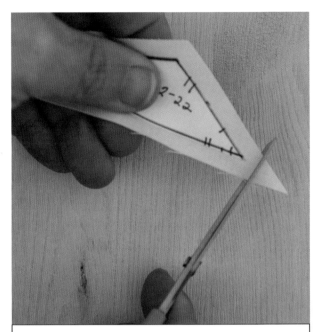

Snip tips off long, pointed facets to reduce bulk on back side of quilt.

 TIP
Cutting Curves

Cutting curved facet edges requires a bit of patience but is very doable.

- Place your ruler along a point on the curve so that the ¼″ measurement is flush with the edge of the freezer paper.

- Set your fabric pencil at the edge of the ruler, delineating the outer edge of the ¼″ seam allowance.

- Slowly pull the ruler down the edge of the freezer paper. Keep the ¼″ measurement flush with the edge of the freezer paper while simultaneously maintaining your fabric pencil at the same spot. By keeping your fabric pencil opposite the point on the freezer paper where the ¼″ measurement is flush with the edge, you will end up drawing a curved line that is parallel to the curved edge of the freezer paper.

- Using scissors or a rotary cutter, follow the curved pencil line to cut an accurate ¼″ seam allowance.

Once you've mastered this technique with your ruler and fabric pencil, try replacing the fabric pencil with your rotary cutter, thereby eliminating a step in the process.

3. Sort your fabric facets by section number (the first number in the unique identifier code) and insert them into their corresponding envelope or baggie.

1. Place the freezer-paper facets on the appropriate color of fabric, leaving at least a ½″ gap between facets.

2. Carefully cut out each fabric facet with a ¼″ seam allowance.

3. Sort the fabric facets by section number and insert them into corresponding envelopes.

Assembling the Facets

In Chapter 3, we discussed how to code your facets to provide visual clues to the piecing order. I called this your Piece Plan (page 67). Now it's time to put that plan into action.

The Piece Plan

Working one section at a time, arrange the fabric facets in the order you'll piece them. Lay the fabric facets on your sewing table in the same configuration as shown on your key.

Identify the individual facets that should be sewn into a single unit. Group those 2 or 3 pieces together by sliding them directly next to one another, perhaps even overlapping a bit. Leave space between these grouped units, providing yet another visual clue to the piecing order.

Lay out facets according to Piece Plan.

Here's an example of how to group the facets:

- Group 5-1 and 5-2.

- Group 5-3 and 5-4, leaving a gap between the previous grouped pieces.

- Group 5-5 and 5-6, leaving a gap between the previous grouped pieces.

- Group 5-7 and 5-8.

- Position 5-9 next to the previous group, leaving a gap between them.

- Group 5-10 and 5-11. (Note that 5-10 and 5-11 are not adjacent to 5-9. This indicates that these pieces should not be sewn together.)

- Position 5-12 next to 5-10 and 5-11, leaving a gap between them.

- Group 5-13 and 5-14.

- Group 5-15 and 5-16, leaving a gap between the previous grouped pieces.

- Position 5-17 next to the previous group, leaving a gap between them.

- Position 5-18 next to 5-17 and the previous group, leaving a gap between them.

Piecing the Facets

Now you are ready to sew your facets together based on the Piece Plan layout. Here's an example of how to assemble the grouped units:

- Sew together 5-1 and 5-2, creating Unit 1:2.

- Sew together 5-3 and 5-4, creating Unit 3:4.

- Sew together Unit 1:2 and Unit 3:4, creating Unit 1:4.

- Sew together 5-5 and 5-6, creating Unit 5:6.

- Sew together 5-7 and 5-8, creating Unit 7:8.

- Sew together Unit 7:8 and 5-9, creating Unit 7:9.

- Sew together Unit 5:6 and Unit 7:9, creating Unit 5:9.

- Sew together Unit 1:4 and Unit 5:9, creating Unit 1:9.

- Sew together 5-10 and 5-11, creating Unit 10:11.

- Sew together 5-12 and Unit 10:11, creating Unit 10:12

- Sew together 5-13 and 5-14, creating Unit 13:14.

- Sew together 5-15 and 5-16, creating Unit 15:16

- Sew together Unit 13:14 and Unit 15:16, creating Unit 13:16.

- Sew together 5-17 to Unit 13:16, creating Unit 13:17.

- Sew together 5-18 to Unit 13:17, creating Unit 13:18.

- Sew together Unit 10:12 and Unit 13:18, creating Unit 10:18

- Sew together Unit 1:9 and Unit 10:18, completing Section 5.

Joining the Freezer-Paper Pieces

1. Select the first 2 fabric facets in your Piece Plan and position them together so that the freezer-paper templates are on the inside of the fabric sandwich, with the edge to be stitched at the top.

2. Holding the 2 fabric facets between your thumb and index finger, with the edge to be sewn at the top, gently pull the fabric closest to you away from its freezer-paper template so you can peek inside the fabric sandwich. Adjust the facets as needed to align the hash marks on either side of the freezer-paper facets. Check that the side corners also match up. If your hash marks and corners do not match, you are trying to piece together 2 fabric facets that don't belong together. Consult your paper key again.

3. Once you are confident that the hash marks and corners align perfectly, carefully pin the 2 facets together in at least 2 places, being careful not to let the facets slip during the process. Place the pins perpendicular to the top edge of the facets.

4. As an alternative to using pins, you can use clips or fabric glue.

5. Sew the 2 facets together by placing the edge of the unit next to the ¼″ seam allowance guide on your needle plate. Then—ever so slightly—move the unit just a needle width to the left. This tiny adjustment prevents you from catching the freezer-paper templates on the inside of the fabric sandwich. You may need to experiment to find the perfect position on your machine.

TIP
Check Your Needles

Quick story: One afternoon I was carefully lining up my needle a hair's width to the left of the ¼″ guide on my machine, but I kept catching the paper every time. Finally, after trying everything else to correct the situation, I changed my needle and voilà—problem resolved! The problem? My needle was bent. The moral to this story? Love and care for your machine's needle.

6. Drop your needle into the fabric a short distance from the top edge and take 1 backstitch to lock the seam. Using a normal stitch length, stitch to the lower edge of the seam and take another backstitch before clipping the threads.

7. Open the pair of fabric facets, now a single unit, and check the freezer-paper placement. Ideally, the 2 freezer-paper templates should float free from the seam, barely touching one another. You should not see any fabric between the edges of your freezer-paper templates at the seamline.

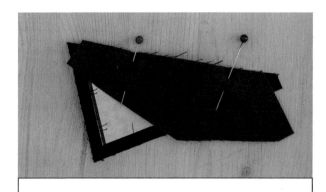

Place pins perpendicular to seamline.

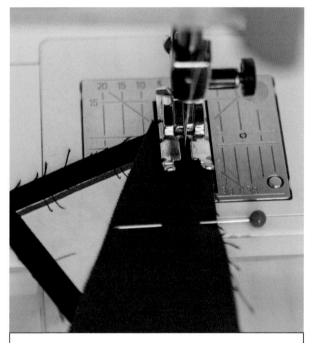

Position facet sandwich a needle width to left of ¼″ line on needle plate.

TIP
To Backstitch or Not to Backstitch?

I learned to backstitch at the start and end of my seams when I first started quilting. It's an old habit. My sewist friends tell me that this can add unwanted bulk to a seam, and that if you use a short stitch length there is no need to back stitch. It's all a matter of personal preference and habit. (I still backstitch.)

If that's not what you see, don't fret! Here are a few things you can do to remedy the situation:

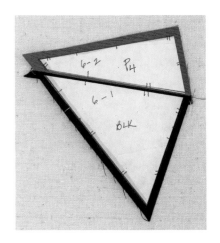

- If you see a bit of fabric on *both sides* of the seam in between the 2 freezer-paper templates, all you need to do is fold the facets back together, place your needle just to the left of the original seam and stitch another seam. Reopen the facets and confirm that the gap is gone.

- If you can see a bit of fabric on only *one side* of the seam (the other side of the freezer-paper template is perfectly aligned to the seam), simply peel the freezer-paper template from the side that has the gap and iron it down with the edge next to the seam. Easy peasy! Be sure to trim the opposite edge down to a ¼″ seam allowance.

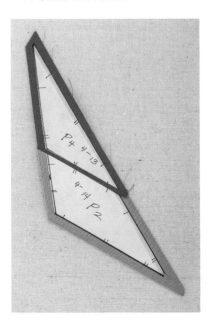

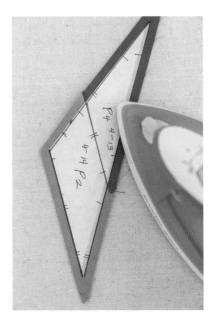

- If a portion of the freezer paper is *barely caught* in the seam, gently tug the seam apart. That might be all it takes to free the paper.

- If a good bit of the freezer paper is *buried* in the seam, consider ripping and resewing. When you bury the freezer paper in the seam allowance, you throw off the edges of the facets. As you can see in the next photo, the left edge of the unit no longer matches up. This will cause problems when you attempt to join the next unit to this one. Position your needle to the right of the original seamline to reduce your chances of catching the freezer paper again.

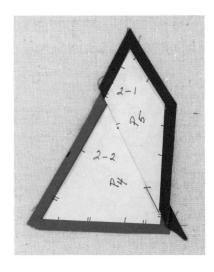

CONSEQUENCES OF GAPS AND TUCKS IN YOUR SEAMS

Burying freezer paper in the seams results in *shortening* that edge of the unit. Leaving gaps in the seams results in *lengthening* the edge of the unit. Both actions impact how well or poorly that unit will line up with the corners and hash marks of the adjacent unit.

But in the end, don't worry about it! Remember in Chapter 3 I mentioned how I purposely design my gems with offset seams. The seams in my gems aren't supposed to match! Light does not follow quilters' rules. No one will know that you have gaps or tucks when they are looking at your gorgeous design.

TIP
Removing Paper Bits

It's okay if a little freezer paper gets stuck in your seam. You know when a bit of the freezer paper is stuck in the seams because it will rip rather away than lift off easily, leaving little bits of paper peeking out of the seam. Simply take a pair of tweezers and gently pull the paper out of the seam from the front.

If the paper won't budge, turn the unit over, open the seams, and remove the paper from between the seam allowance. And if that doesn't work, take the business end of a seam ripper and shove those little bits of paper from the right side back down inside the seam.

8. Gently press the seams to one side without stretching the edges of the facet. I decide which side to press the seams depending on how flat they will lay.

- If there are more intersecting seams on one side of the seamline than on the other, I'll press the seam to the side with fewer intersecting seams.

- If a seam includes the long edge of a needle-nose facet, I try to press the seam away from the tip of the needle-nose facet so that it lies flat. Invariably, when I try to press the seam allowance of a needle-nose facet back under itself, the facet may twist and not lie flat.

- If it makes no difference which side I press, I press seams toward the darkest fabric.

- In some cases, the seam lies flattest when I make a little slit in the seam allowance and press one part of the seam allowance to one side, and the other to the opposite side. This technique is best used for quilts that will be used for display purposes. I wouldn't advise cutting seam allowances for functional quilts, particularly if they are going to be regularly laundered. Since I don't put my art quilts in the washer, I use this technique liberally to help my seams lay flat.

9. Once you've pieced a section together, baste around the edges to help prevent it from stretching.

Managing Special Challenges

Freezer-paper piecing can be used to translate nearly any design into a quilt. In some cases, our designs include some piecing challenges. Here are a few suggestions to manage some of the most common ones.

Set-In Seams (Y-seams)

Set-in seams occur when 3 facets and 3 seams join in 1 spot. The 3 seams coming together create the shape of the capital letter Y. Most seams in quilting are sewn edge to edge, but set-in seams are the exception. These seams must start and stop exactly ¼″ from the edge of the fabric where all 3 seams meet.

1. Lay 2 of the 3 pieces one on top of the other, right sides together, so that the corner where the Y-seam will occur is on the left. With your fabric pencil or pen, mark exactly ¼″ from the left edge of the seamline. Starting at this point, drop your needle into the mark and lock the stitch (don't backstitch, since that will eliminate your precise ¼″ gap). Stitch to the opposite edge. Open the pair of facets so that right sides are facing up. Press your seam under the lower facet.

2. Pivot the pair of facets clockwise. Lay the third facet onto the edge of the previously sewn pair, right sides together, so that the spot where all 3 seams come together is once again on the left. With your fabric pencil, mark exactly ¼″ from the left edge. Starting at this point, drop your needle into the mark and lock the stitch. Stitch to the opposite edge. Open the facet and press the seam under the upper facet.

2 Y-seams in Emerald Birthstone block

3. You now have all 3 facets pressed open with right sides facing up. 2 of the seams are complete. To finish the third seam, fold down the top half of the trio of facets so that the 2 unsewn edges now align. The point at which the Y-seam comes together is again on your left. Having accurately started your line of stitching ¼″ away from the edge of the last 2 seams, you now have a nice visual clue where to drop your needle. Place your needle at the very edge of the line of stitching and lock the stitch. Sew to the opposite edge. Open the facets and press the seam to the side that allows the facets to lie flat.

Needle-Nose Facets

Keep an eye on the tips of facets that come to a long and narrow point at the end. I call these *needle-nose facets*. They have a tendency to twist away from the presser foot when you're sewing towards them, preventing the unit from lying flat.

The best way to handle these long, pointy facets is to begin your line of stitching from the skinniest end and stitch down to the widest end. If you have no choice but to start your stitching from the widest end, slow your stitch speed and hold the needle-nose facet in place with your finger as you approach it.

Once sewn, press the seam away from the skinny end of the needle-nose facet. This helps it lie straight and flat. If you press the seam under the skinny end, your needle-nose facet may twist and warp.

Curves

You can add curves to the design and still use freezer-paper piecing techniques to create your quilt. However, you must remove the freezer paper before pinning and sewing the curve. Therefore, it's important that you extend each hash mark from the edge of the freezer-paper template into the seam allowance *before* removing the freezer paper.

After drawing hash marks into the seam allowance and removing the freezer paper, lay the convex curved piece (the hill) on top of the concave curved piece (the valley) so that they meet at the middle center point. Pin at this point. (*Convex curves* are

defined as having an outline or surface curved like the *exterior* of a circle or sphere. *Concave curves* are defined as having an outline or surface curved like the *interior* of a circle or sphere.) Some experts recommend clipping the concave seam at ¼″ intervals, but often the bias edge of the fabric makes it just as easy to ease in the seams without clipping.

Working along the seam on either side of the pinned center point, match up the hash marks on the inside of the seam allowance and pin along the seamline.

Position the convex facet (the piece that lays flat) on the bottom of the fabric sandwich. Use your fingers to smooth the fabric on the top facet before it slides under your needle. Small puckers can be smoothed out, but pleats must be unstitched and resewn.

Small Facets

Want to know the best way to deal with small facets? Simply breathe. These little pieces can cause us the most frustration, especially those of us with a bit of arthritis in our hands. Yet they are very powerful additions to your design, because they provide the bling. Here are a few tips for managing small pieces:

1. Cut out one section of your design at a time. This reduces the number of tiny freezer-paper facets you need to worry about.

2. Be sure to drop each freezer-paper facet into the appropriately labeled envelope immediately after cutting.

3. Static electricity can cause freezer-paper pieces to stick to the inside of the envelope or to each other. After removing the freezer-paper facets from the envelope, check inside the envelope to ensure every single facet has been removed. Also check the back side (the waxy side) of every large freezer-paper facet to make sure that a little facet hasn't become stuck there.

4. Breath. Stretch often. Pay attention to your shoulders. Are they inching up toward your ears? Maybe that's a good time to take a little break and let them relax. Regard these little freezer-paper facets as your friends!

Converging Seams

In Chapter 3, I suggested that you offset your seams so that they don't collide into one another at a single point. In some cases, though, offsetting seams won't achieve the desired affect you want in your design. Here are a few tips to manage converging seams.

1. Trim seam allowances to reduce bulk.

2. Press seams in the same direction so that they overlap.

3. Use a pressing tool to help seams lie flat and straight, reducing bulk.

Project: Piece the Freezer-Paper Pieces

Finished Mozambique purple garnet, *Lovely Laurie*

1. Working one section at a time, arrange the facets in the order in which you'll piece them together. Consult your paper key.

2. Position pairs of fabric facets together along their shared edge using the hash marks to ensure alignment.

3. Sew together each pair of facets (with right sides facing one another) into a unit with a seam allowance that is a needle-width shy of ¼″ to avoid catching the freezer paper.

4. Press the seams to the side that will allow the unit to lie flat.

5. Do not remove the freezer-paper template from the fabric facet until after you have extended the hash marks into the seam allowance, preserving the important visual clue that will help you assemble the sections together.

6. Once a section is complete, stitch around the edges to prevent them from stretching.

7. Sew all sections together.

CHAPTER 5

Quilting and Finishing Your Gem

Detail of *Lila* (page 102), from the Angle of Repose series
Photo by Tony Bennett Photography

Quilting Techniques

One of the most difficult challenges in developing my gem quilts was deciding how to quilt them. I spend most of my time ensuring that the flow of light and color across the facets of my gems is just right. I don't want to distract a viewer with quilting that adds an additional, unnecessary layer of design to the work.

I tried to quilt my early gem quilts by hand with a traditional quilt stitch, but the thickness of the seams made it difficult to push a needle through the fabric. Not only were my stitches uneven, my hands ached. I also knew that I wouldn't be able to hand quilt the giant gem portraits that were in my imagination, so I decided to experiment with machine quilting.

My first attempt at machine quilting was to outline each of the major facets on *Communion* (page 97). The result was less than desirable. The quilt looked like a rumpled sheet! I realized I needed to figure out a better quilting pattern that accomplished the following:

- Acted as a screen through which the viewer would see the flow of light and color in my gem, rather than distract them with yet another design element.

- Gobbled up the fullness that sometimes occurs when sewing irregular pieces together.

- Allowed me to relax and have fun while quilting my work.

Hand Embellishment

Embellishing the surface with decorative stitches is one way to add texture to your quilt. I decided to use this technique after watching wonderful artists create interesting work at a weekend retreat. I returned home, ripped out the machine quilting from *Communion* (page 97), and began a months-long process of embellishing each facet with decorative stitches. I loved that process! I spent several joyful months working with the quilt in a lap hoop, moving indoors and outdoors depending on the weather.

I have to admit that I was sad when I decided that the embellishment was finished. I loved the time I spent meditatively working gorgeous embroidery thread throughout her facets. However, I also knew that I'd have to live to be 400 years old to finish all the quilts I wanted to create if I used that technique.

As a result, I decided to try my hand again at a quilting pattern that met all the criteria of acting as a screen, gobbling up fullness, and allowing me to relax and have fun as I quilted.

Detail of hand stitching on *Communion* (page 97)

Machine Quilting

After trial and error, I developed a random, nondirectional pattern of machine quilting that met all my criteria. The nested flame shape that I use to quilt my gems is incredibly flexible and forgiving.

The goal is to create shapes of varied lengths, widths, and direction. Unlike traditional quilting patterns, there is no discernible pattern, so your eye immediately looks past it to the underlying surface and piecing designs. Unlike stippling, you can cross over an existing line of quilting, allowing maximum movement across the facet.

Detail of *Blush* (page 98) filled with wild-motion machine quilting in each facet

Practicing Wild-Motion Machine Quilting

I've nicknamed my technique "wild-motion machine quilting" and it is easy to learn. Spend some time doodling shapes by hand before trying them on your domestic machine. This will help your brain understand the shapes intuitively before adding the pressure that comes from sitting in front of a machine.

Practice the following shapes with a pen or pencil on a sheet of paper. Don't worry about making all the shapes identical. That's not the point. The point is to get your brain familiar with the components of the shape from different directions so that you can eventually create them with ease at your machine.

- Draw a flame shape starting at the bottom, moving up the left side with a swooping shape ending at the tip, and then falling back to the right with a soft crescent shape, ending at the base.

- Draw a flame shape starting at the bottom, moving up the right side with a swooping shape ending at the tip, and then falling back to the left with a soft crescent shape, ending at the base.

- Draw a flame shape starting at the top, moving down the right side with a swooping shape ending at the tip, and then sweeping back up the left side with a soft crescent shape.

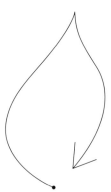

Practice Shape 1: Up left, down right.

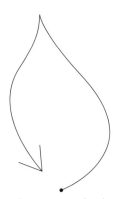

Practice Shape 2: Up right, down left.

Practice Shape 3: Down right, up left.

- Draw a flame shape starting at the top, moving down the left side with a swooping shape ending at the tip, and then sweeping back up the right side with a soft crescent shape.

- Draw a flame shape starting at the left side, moving over the top with a swooping shape ending at the tip at the right. Then draw a soft crescent shape under the form ending at the left.

- Draw a flame shape starting at the left side, dipping below with a swooping shape ending at the tip at the right. Then draw a soft crescent shape over the top ending at the left.

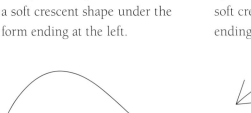

Practice Shape 5: Top right, bottom left.

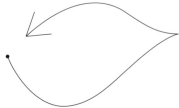

Practice Shape 6: Bottom right, top left.

Practice Shape 4: Down left, up right.

- Draw a flame shape starting at the right side, moving over the top with a swooping shape ending at the tip at the left. Then draw a soft crescent shape under the form ending at the right.

Practice Shape 7: Top left, bottom right.

- Draw a flame shape starting at the right side, dipping below with a swooping shape ending at the tip at the left. Then draw a soft crescent shape over the top ending at the right.

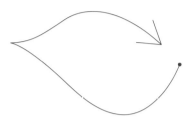

Practice Shape 8: Bottom left, top right.

- Draw a cluster of flame shapes that flare out in 4 different directions.

Practice Shape 9: Four-blossom cluster.

- Draw a series of rectangles and triangles on a sheet of paper. Fill the shapes with flame shapes that are linked, intertwine, and nest together. Feel free to cross existing lines. Make the shapes various sizes and point in various directions on purpose. Fill the space!

Practice Shape 10: Nestled cluster.

Once you feel confident with these shapes, assemble 4 or 5 fabric sandwiches (top, batting, and batting) on which to practice. Before putting the fabric sandwich under your needle, draw several large triangle and quadrilateral shapes on it using a pen. Now put the sandwich under your needle and practice filling these shapes with the flame shapes of all different sizes and pointing all different directions. Have fun!

Finishing Your Gem

Gallery Facings with Mitered Corners

I have made over 300 quilts in my 30 years as a quiltmaker, and I typically have added traditional bindings to each one. However, when I learned how to add gallery facings to my quilts, I knew this was the technique I would use going forward. I love the clean, artistic edge and how professional the quilt looks hanging on the wall.

1. Trim the raw edges of your quilt to the desired finished size plus ¼˝.

2. Cut facing strips 2½˝ wide for each of the 4 edges of your quilt. The length of the strip should be 4˝ longer than the length of the side on which it will be sewn. This will give you an overlap of 2˝ on either side of the quilt edge.

3. On the wrong side of a strip, turn up a ¼˝ hem and press.

4. Lay the unfolded edge of a strip along the *front edge* of your quilt. Mark each end of the strip in 2 places: at the very edge of your quilt and ¼˝ in from the edge of the quilt.

5. Pin the strip to the quilt. Place your last pin at the ¼˝ mark that you made in Step 5.

6. From the front side, stitch through all layers using a ¼˝ seam allowance, starting and ending at the ¼˝ inside marks.

7. Pull back the end of the strip you just sewed to keep it out of the way of the adjacent strip you will sew next. Repeat Steps 3–6 for the remaining strips. The stitching should meet at the ¼˝ mark inside the edge but not overlap.

8. Fold the free edge of the strip back over itself to create a 45° angle to the corner point of the quilt. Press to create a crease. This will serve as a guide over which you'll pin and sew to get a mitered corner.

9. Bring the 2 folded edges of the quilt together so that the creased folds align. Pull the quilt away from the strips to get it out of the way of the pins. Pin along the creased line.

10. Sew from the folded edge of the strip to the quilt. Be sure to turn the quilt edges away from the stitch line so that they don't get caught in the mitered seam.

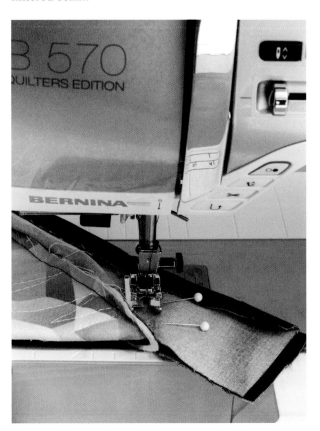

11. Remove the bulk in the corner by clipping in 3 places: Clip off the dog-ears from the strips, clip off the corner of the quilt sandwich, and trim the quilt edge so that it tapers to the corner.

12. Repeat Steps 8–11 for the remaining corners.

13. Turn the quilt to the front and press the facing strips away from the quilt top. You won't be able to press all the way to the corner due to the pocket formed by the mitered edge.

14. On the front side of the quilt, with the facing strip pressed away from the quilt top, place a line of stitching just a needle width to the right of the seamline. You'll sew through the facing and the seam allowance of the quilt underneath the facing. This will help you turn the facing cleanly to the back in the next step.

15. Turn the facing to the back of the quilt and gently push each corner to a point. Work the facing to the back with just a smidge of the quilt top showing at the edge. Pin the pressed edge in place and hand-stitch the folded edge of the facing to the quilt.

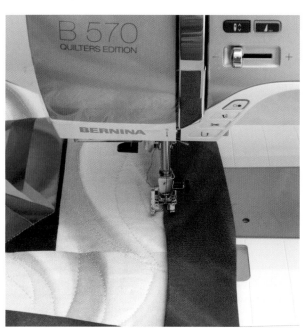
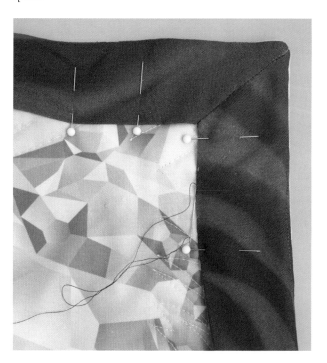

Labels

I always create labels for my quilts. Our quilts are important artifacts that will hopefully last many years. It's important that we preserve information about the maker, the inspiration, the date / time period, and perhaps the story of why this quilt was created. You are creating art; label it!

Rod Sleeves

I add 2 sleeves to my finished quilts: one at the top for the hanging rod, and one below for a wooden slat that helps straighten and stabilize the bottom edge. I add the rod and lower sleeves after I've completed the gallery facing. The technique I use to create a gallery sleeve is described below.

1. Cut a 9½"-wide strip the length of the top edge of your quilt.

2. Turn the short ends ¼" to the wrong side of the fabric. Do this twice to create a finished edge.

3. Fold the strip lengthwise with wrong sides together; press the folded edge.

4. Open the strip so that it lies flat with the wrong side facing up. Fold one long edge of the strip so that it meets the center crease; do the same with the other side. Press the folded edges to create sharp creases.

5. Fold the strip lengthwise along your original center crease so that the wrong sides are together. Sew the raw edges together with a ¼" seam allowance. (This will look weird, since we're used to sewing fabric with the right sides together.) Press the seam open.

6. Place the sleeve at the top edge of the quilt back with the center seam down, facing the quilt.

7. Find the 2 creases you created earlier. These will be the edges of your sleeve, providing plenty of fullness on the front to accommodate display poles or slats. Position one of the creases about ½″ below the top edge of your quilt. Pin at one corner, pin at the opposite corner, and then pin in between the 2. Find the second crease and pin accordingly.

8. Stitch the sleeve in place by hand.

9. Repeat Steps 1–8 to create your second sleeve for the bottom of your quilt.

Storage

I store my quilts on a rolled tube inside of a drawstring sleeve made of outdoor fabric. I create a label that I fuse to the outside of the quilt bag that lists the name of the quilt, the size, and my full contact information.

In addition, I add a tag that hangs from the top with the same information. Since I store my quilts at the top of a shelf with the ends visible, it's much easier to identify each quilt with the end tag than having to pull each one off the shelf to read the bag label. Both are necessary!

Project: Finishing Your Gem

1. Create your fabric backing and layer it with batting and your quilt top.

2. Pin baste all 3 layers together using large safety pins. Place pins no more than 7″ apart.

3. Quilt your gem using a design you love. I prefer to use my Flickering Flame pattern or a tight stipple. However, straight lines running parallel or diagonal across the surface of your gem also look lovely. Try using a very thin thread (high thread weight) in a neutral color so that it disappears into your quilt.

4. Trim your quilt to within ¼″ of the desired size.

5. Add a gallery facing or traditional binding to your quilt.

6. Add a rod sleeve and a lower sleeve to stabilize the quilt if you wish.

7. Create a label that includes the name of the quilt; its dimensions; your name, location, and date; and any other pertinent information you would like people to know about your work.

8. Create a drawstring storage bag. Fuse a label to the front that includes details of the quilt plus all your contact information. Finally, attach a tag to the end of the drawstring that also includes details of the quilt and your contact information.

PART III

GALLERIES

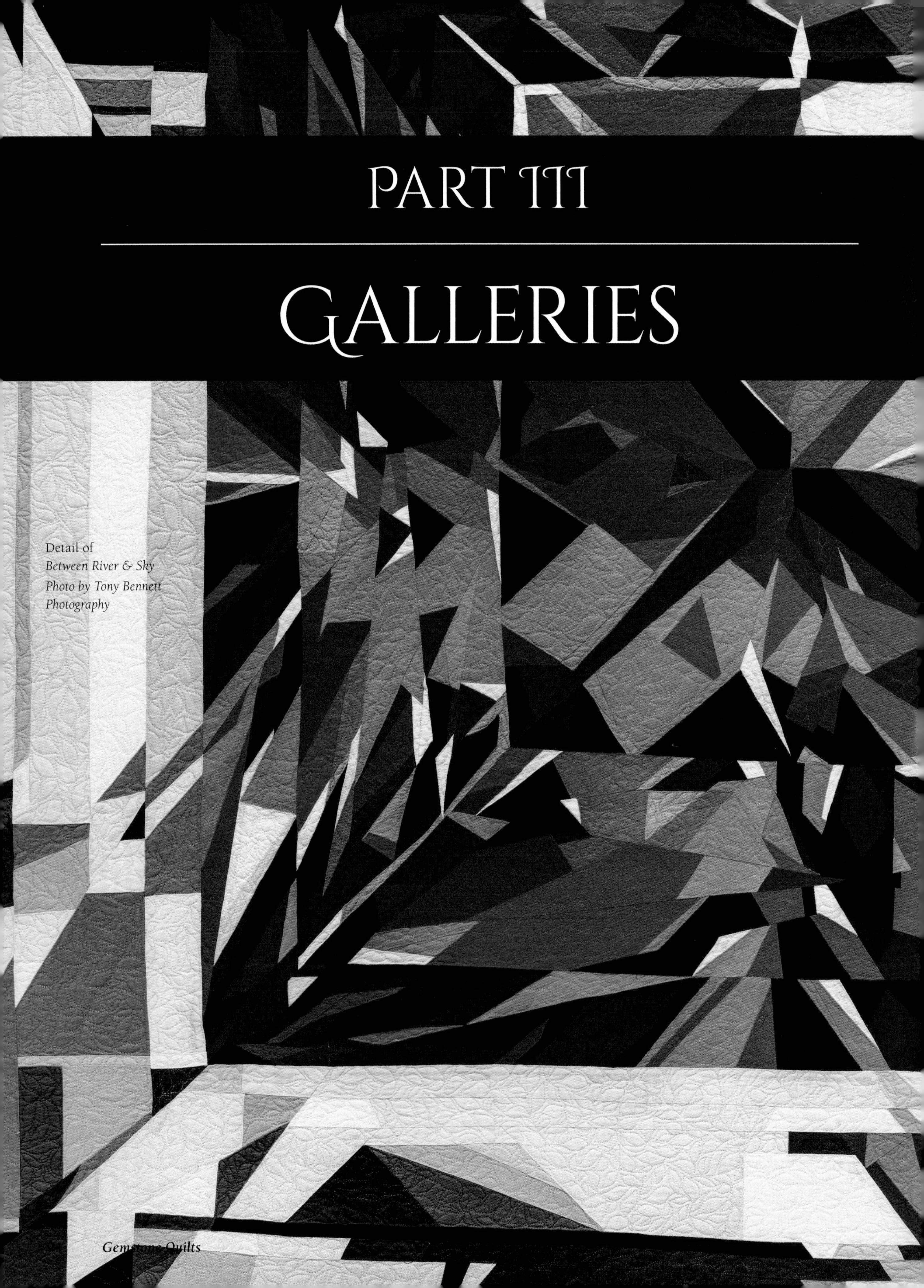

Detail of
Between River & Sky
Photo by Tony Bennett
Photography

Solitaire, 54″ × 54″, 1998.
*Techniques: Freezer-paper pieced
with solid fabrics, hand quilted.*

Roses for Sister Eilerman,
52″ × 58″, 1999.
*Techniques: Freezer-paper pieced
with printed fabrics, hand quilted.*

Penumbra, *50″ × 52″, 2001.*
Techniques: Freezer-paper pieced with
hand-dyed fabrics, hand quilted.

Nikki's Wedding Quilt,
36″ × 36″, 2002.
Techniques: Freezer-paper pieced
with batik fabrics, hand quilted.

Communion,
55″ × 77″, 2013,
from the Angle of
Repose series.
Techniques: Freezer-
paper pieced with
hand-painted fabrics,
hand embellished.

Blush, *55″ × 85″, 2014,
from the Angle of
Repose series.
Techniques: Freezer-
paper pieced with
hand-painted fabrics,
machine quilted.*

Eclipse 2020, *60″ × 60″, 2020
Techniques: Freezer-paper
pieced with hand-painted and
solid fabrics, machine quilted.*

*Photo courtesy of the
International Quilt Museum,
University of Nebraska-Lincoln*

Devil's Due, 53″ × 78″, 2016, from the Bourbon Diamonds series. Techniques: Freezer-paper pieced with hand-painted and printed fabrics, machine quilted.

Angel's Share, 58″ × 58″, 2016,
from the Bourbon Diamonds series.
Techniques: Freezer-paper pieced with hand-
painted and printed fabrics, machine quilted.

Fire & Ice, *50″ × 82″, 2016,*
from the Bourbon Diamonds series.
Techniques: Freezer-paper pieced with
hand-painted fabrics, machine quilted.

Old-Fashioned New, *46″ × 82″, 2017,*
from the Bourbon Diamonds series.
Techniques: Freezer-paper pieced with
hand-painted fabrics, machine quilted.

Kentucky Honey, *42″ × 52″, 2016, from the Bourbon Diamonds series.*
Techniques: Freezer-paper pieced with hand-painted fabrics, machine quilted.

Copper Queen, *44″ × 67″, 2017, from the Bourbon Diamonds series.*
Techniques: Freezer-paper pieced with hand-painted fabrics, machine quilted.

Lila, 58″ × 58″, 2017, from the Angle of Repose series.
Techniques: Freezer-paper pieced with solid fabrics, machine quilted.

Char #4, 48″ × 81″, 2017, from the Bourbon Diamonds series.
Techniques: Freezer-paper pieced with hand-painted fabrics, machine quilted.
Photo by Cliff Patrie

Maker's Flame, *50″ × 105″, 2018,
from the Bourbon Diamonds series.
Made with the assistance of
Amy Del Grosso and Bonnie Taylor.
Techniques: Freezer-paper pieced
with solid and hand-painted fabrics,
machine quilted.*

Photo by Tony Bennett Photography

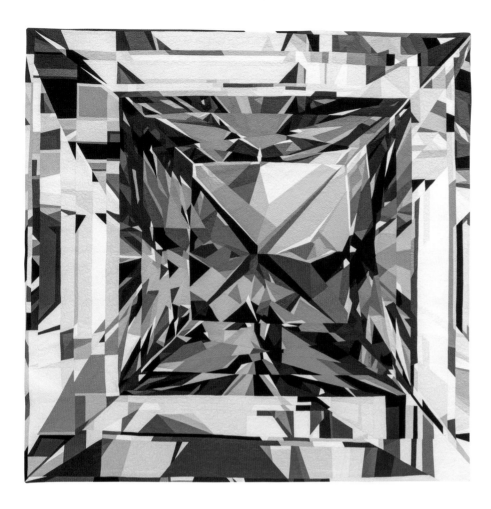

Between River & Sky, 69″ × 71″, 2018,
from the Bourbon Diamonds series.
Made with the assistance of
Amy Del Grosso and Bonnie Taylor.
Techniques: Freezer-paper pieced with
solid fabrics, machine quilted.

The Peace Quilt, 84″ × 86″, 2019.
Made with the assistance of
Amy Del Grosso and Bonnie Taylor.
Techniques: Freezer-paper pieced
with solid and hand-painted
fabrics, machine quilted.
Photo by Tony Bennett Photography

Enlightened, 38½″ × 38½″, by Linda Fisher. Techniques: Freezer-paper pieced with printed fabrics, machine quilted.

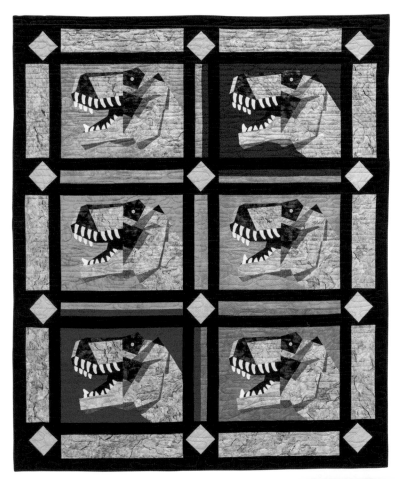

The Mighty T-Rex, *62″ × 72″,*
by Annette Fry.
Techniques: Freezer-paper piecing and
wool appliqué with printed fabrics,
machine quilted.

Dominus Flevit, *37″ × 49″,*
by Julia Graves.
Techniques: Freezer-paper piecing
and fused appliqué with printed
fabrics, machine quilted.

Tree of Life, 46″ × 62″, by Julia Graves. Techniques: Freezer-paper piecing with printed fabrics, machine quilted.

Infinity Combined, *36″ × 36″*,
by Karen M. Bailey.
Techniques: Freezer-paper piecing
with solid fabrics, machine quilted.

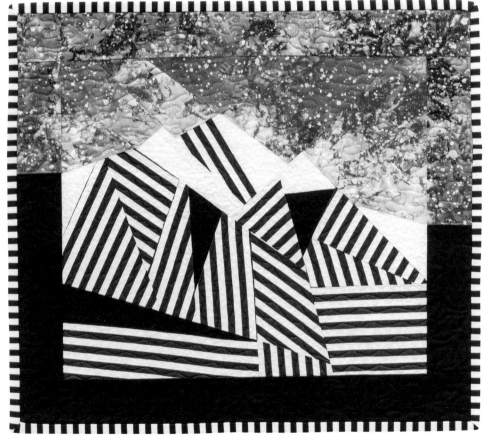

Mountain Jewel, *16″ × 18″*,
by Jimeen A. Thurston.
Techniques: Freezer-paper
piecing with printed fabrics,
machine quilted.

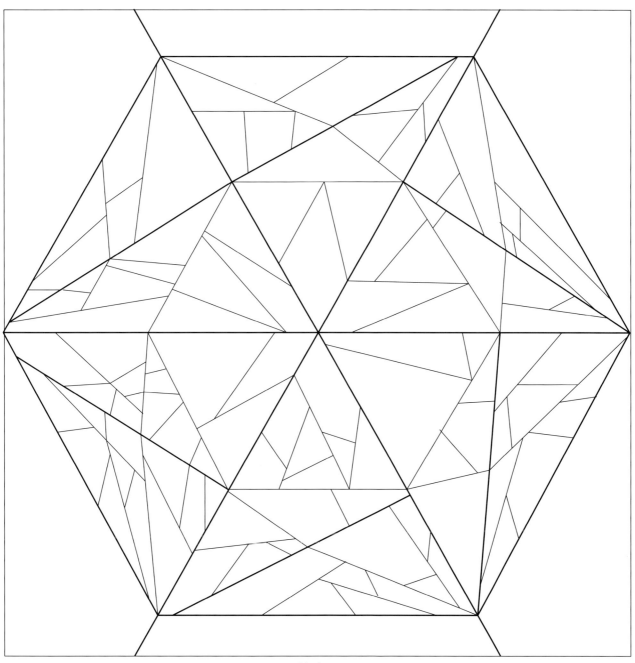

Mock-up

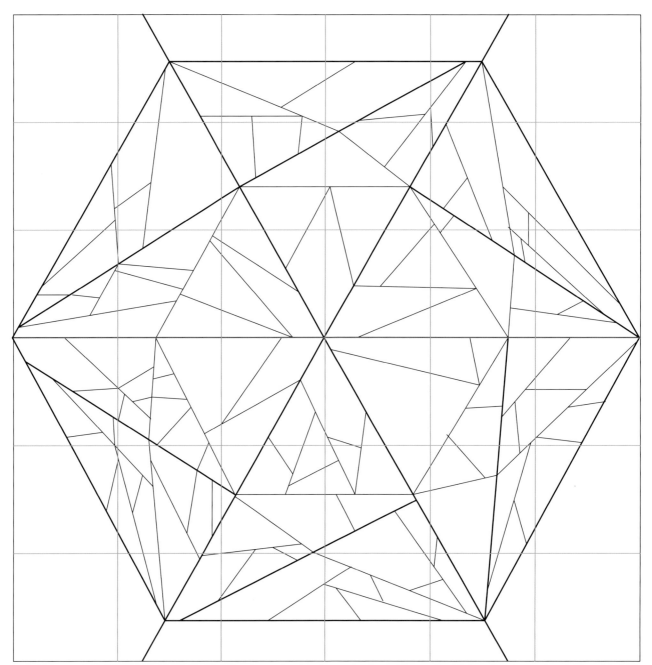

Mock-up with grid

About the Author

MJ Kinman likes to tell people that she makes the biggest diamonds in the world. The adventure started over twenty years ago when an image of a gem captured her imagination. As a new quiltmaker, she knew there had to be a way to transform that image into a quilt, but she didn't know where to begin. After seven years of research, MJ made her first gem quilt.

Her current series is based on the National Gem Collection at the Smithsonian's National Museum of Natural History. Her previous series, entitled Bourbon Diamonds, celebrates Kentucky's favorite spirit and most popular export.

MJ's work has been exhibited in international shows, galleries, and museums, including the International Quilt Museum (Lincoln, Nebraska) and The National Quilt Museum (Paducah, Kentucky). Quiltmakers have read about her work in *Quilting Arts Magazine*, *Quiltfolk*, *Les Nouvelles—Patchwork et Création Textile*, *McCall's Quilting*, *Make Modern* magazine, *Online Quilt Magazine*, and *World Diamond Magazine*. Viewers of *Quilting Arts TV* and *The Quilt Show with Alex Anderson and Ricky Tims* have learned about MJ's practice and process. Her gem quilts are included in private collections, including Maker's Mark Distillery (Loretto, Kentucky).

MJ released her first pattern series in 2018. The Birthstone series is a collection of twelve blocks representing the traditional birthstones. Her Diamond Divas series features larger quilt patterns inspired by fancy-cut diamonds. She and Northcott have collaborated on several collections featuring her unique gemstone designs.

MJ loves to teach others how to use freezer-paper piecing techniques in order to bring their own inspiration to life. She launched a teacher certification program in 2018. Gem Affiliates are independent teachers around the world who are certified to teach her patterns.

Photo by Michelle Ann Morris

Visit MJ online and follow on social media!

Website: mjkinman.com

Facebook: /mjkinmantextileartist

Instagram: @mjkinman_textileartist